Christian Faith in Our Time

FRITZ BURI

Christian Faith in Our Time

Translated by

EDWARD ALLEN KENT

THE MACMILLAN COMPANY, NEW YORK

COLLIER-MACMILLAN LIMITED, LONDON

Contents

CONTENTS

Translator's Preface

By his own account the author's views have shifted some-what since the original publication of this brief study of "Christain faith in our time." Nevertheless, even this "token" analysis offers a challenge to those who would settle too easily for a theology of revelation, and perhaps more important, the promise of renewed engagement between faith and reason—a new direction towards a rational faith—to those who would not, or could not, abandon "the gift of reason" in the pursuit of honest faith.

This translation follows the German except for an occasional "Englishing" of obscure literary images. The RSV has been employed except for one or two instances in which the King James text more accurately rendered the intent of the allusion.

EDWARD ALLEN KENT

Vassar College

Foreword

This study represents the slightly edited text of a series of lectures intended to communicate to a lay audience some impression of the present theological climate and the role that can be played in it by liberal theology. What I advocate as liberal theology is not simply the version of an earlier era, no longer adequate to our current experience and altered cultural situation—a situation which has seen the radical readjustment of our collective consciousness. Despite some assumptions common to the liberal theology of the nineteenth and twentieth centuries, the present genre is a new creation—otherwise it would be as dead as many have found its predecessor.

Liberal theology still survives, and in forms which are not entirely anachronistic—such as I hope to present here. Still the designation "liberal" is not of crucial import, but rather the discovery of some authentic way to guide Christian theology out of the spiritual chaos of our time—whatever this way be called. That this way does not lie through present-day protestant orthodoxy should be readily apparent from that theology's disastrous capitulation to current nihilism—a capitulation whose causes I shall examine in what follows. In fact, an appraisal of the consequences of orthodoxy as well as an evaluation of the legitimate concerns of nihilism is perhaps the special calling of a renewed liberal tradition. It seems to me, at least, that "liberal" is the perspective from which the proclamation of the Bible must be understood today, and that liberalism is the means by which Christian faith in our time can be made viable.

I hope that those who heard my Bernoulli lectures will find this exposition of interest, for it centers on the issues most debated in them. Not for the last time do I hope to render that audience an opportunity to examine the import of the lectures in detail, and to evaluate the assumptions underlying what it heard from my lectern. I think also of my students, who will find here a concise compilation of what I have sought to develop for them in other forms and contexts.

In the text references have been made to earlier as well as present-day theological positions in footnotes located near the statements suggested by these sources. Hopefully these notes will give theologians as well as non-theologians occasion and opportunity to pursue further what is developed in this work only in briefest form.

Friends as well as critics may consider this preliminary study as a token pledge towards a future comprehensive account of what is sketched here in broad outline. I am aware that I may be preaching to deaf ears. But I hope to win some consideration for my views, especially among those who have paid only lip service to the Christian faith as it has been presented to them thus far. Above all I have tried to let myself be led by the Word: "Break up your fallow ground and sow not among thorns."

FRITZ BURI

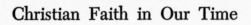

Christian Faith in Our Time

One

THE FACE OF

OUR TIME

✦

Our general concern—Christian faith in our time—might be approached by either of two fundamentally different methods. One, assuming an impartial point of view, would attempt an objective survey of the current status of Christian belief, its distinctive manifestations and consequences, and also, the hostile forces and movements ranged against it. The other, speaking from within the faith, would use these same thematic elements as a basis for an assessment of what remains valid in Christianity after its confrontation with non-Christian viewpoints—and thus not only offer an analysis of the present status of the faith, but further, propose what we ought to believe.

But in fact, our topic cannot be treated adequately by either of these methods alone: neither an objective and thus uncommitted account nor a confessional appeal which in return solicits personal decision is sufficient for our task. Both methods must be utilized, the one supplementing the other.

For regardless of what aspect of the Christian faith is examined, those ideologies which would oppose it must be given due consideration—whether or not one judges such ideologies legitimate, whether or not one wants to deal with them at all. Issues are at stake in the encounter of belief with nonbelief that cannot be left in abeyance, and to disclaim any statement on such issues is really to claim no more than a standoff position. If we are to deal honestly with the questions raised by Christian faith in our time, and to win clarity for our own position, we must press beyond such disengagement.

Precisely because we are determined to clarify our personal situations, and because we must try to avoid the pitfall of a premature and baseless personal commitment—whether positive or negative—we cannot settle for a simple confession, no matter how sincerely felt nor historically powerful it may seem to be at the moment. The very diversity of confessional pronouncements with which the Christian faith confronts us— whether it be the confessions of individuals or of whole groups and churches—demands that we analyze them critically and, moreover, the problems which they raise. Unless it is subjected to critical examination, our faith cannot speak to the real dilemmas of our troubled age.

Thus our analysis proceeds from questions: What can Christian faith be in our time? What should it be? No such analysis can be elicited immediately from traditional confessions, nor would it be appropriate to expound merely personal views and beliefs. Nor can the Bible itself be expected to provide a sufficient basis for our investigation, since its texts must inevitably be approached with the biases of our own time. Instead, let us begin by directly examining the time in which we live, let us study particularly the "face" of our time.

This figure—the face of our time—is intended to emphasize that our primary interest lies not so much in our external heritage and destiny as in our collective "personality," in how our generation sees itself. For it is perhaps the distinctive characteristic of the human countenance that it is not only formed by external factors and inner necessities but also reveals how an individual comprehends himself and feels himself to be situated within the world of his experience. The face is the unique expression of spiritual and intellectual self-consciousness.

In speaking of the face of our time—by necessity an anonymous face—we cannot hope to characterize the entire mind of our epoch. Yet if we cannot reckon the whole, we can consider its distinctive exponents—and insofar as we are members of this common intellectual environment, although not as individuals identical with it, we will perhaps be able to achieve a clearer understanding of ourselves and of one another. For the face of our time is in part the face of each of us, the expression of our self-awareness, of that interior locus of understanding where, with all our differences, we may find some shared basis for agreement.

What we are about can be formulated now, as it was for his age, by those incisive and all-encompassing questions of Kant, expressed in the *Critique of Pure Reason:* [1]

> What can I know?
> What ought I to do?
> What may I hope?

These three questions will be useful in the analysis of the face of our time because they offer an apt matrix for fixing the significance of Christian faith, for analyzing its distinctive claims and its critical opposition, and for discovering what assumptions this faith shares with alien viewpoints. In the context of these questions, three points will be stressed: first, the face of our time has undergone a radical transformation from that of the previous era—despite their close temporal proximity; second, in its attitude toward Christian faith, the face of our time is manifestly torn, rent by inner tensions; third, Christian faith today seems as much in accord with anti-Christianity in some crucial respects as it is unrelated in others—an accord which must be considered extremely ominous. Special attention in this study, whose findings we are perhaps already anticipating, will be devoted to the reasons for the basic change in the temper of our age, and especially to those novel features of our

[1] "Transcendental Doctrine of Method," Chap. 2, Sec. 2, trans. by Norman Kemp Smith (London, Macmillan and Co., 1953), p. 635.

own *visage* which can be contrasted with that of the preceding era.

There are four perspectives from which we shall appoach the face of our time. Let us begin by examining

1   The face of the time from which our own derives.

Applying the schema of Kantian questions recommended above, we are immediately struck by

A   *An unprecedented confidence in science in response to the question, What can I know?*

In his *Critique,* Kant prescribed boundaries for reason which prohibited its use in the construction of speculative world views—boundaries inherent in its own structure. According to Kant, natural cognition was valid only when circumscribed within the sphere of human experience; when reason was extended beyond this limit, it was lured into contradictory and deceptive speculations. Thus Kant believed he had refuted, once and for all, those so-called proofs of God by which it had been thought possible to deduce God's existence from the concept of his perfect being, his necessity as first cause, and his role as wise author of the world from its rational design.

Yet discrepancies were subsequently discovered in the Kantian critique of reason, and also Kant himself disclosed new possibilities for metaphysical speculation. Shortly after Kant, new idealistic philosophies were propounded which, despite some novel perspectives, reinstated the old proofs of God on their original foundations—God again seemed to be of central import to reason. The relationship of theology to philosophy and science was reestablished, and concomitantly, simple piety clung to its assumption that it would be unreasonable not to believe in God and unreasonable not to recognize the creator in his works.

At the same time, and now liberated by its appeal to Kant's restriction of reason to pure concepts and the realm of human experience, a science evolved which would recognize nothing attributed to a higher spiritual reality—nor would this science acknowledge that Kant had provided alternative routes to religious understanding. As compensation for their rejection of the supernatural, scientists accomplished diverse technological wonders: benefiting both themselves and their society, they made extensive progress in the investigation of the natural sphere. With great enthusiasm their champions proclaimed: "There is no world but that known and explained by science; and what does not adapt itself to the views of modern science is pure fancy." Thus, while idealism was claiming that it could vindicate God scientifically, materialism was countering that it could scientifically disprove him.

Scandalized by materialistic repudiation of God but lacking confidence in the idealistic proofs, a long succession of theologians sought to agree on some new way to rescue the faith. Yet Kant had indicated the proper course when he declared: "I must deny knowledge in order to make room for faith." [2] But if Kant had grounded faith in ethics, he had, nevertheless, derived it from irrational experience. Reason, he had suggested, is not appropriate to the sphere of religious experience; faith requires a mode of experience which presupposes the validity of religious conviction as the fulfillment of basic needs of the

[2] *Critique of Pure Reason,* preface to 2d ed., p. 29.

human spirit. In Kant's wake followed other attempts to justify this peculiarity scientifically, especially since Christian faith irrupts into the dimension of history through the figure of Jesus. Yet such "theology of experience" depended entirely upon the ability to prove that one was dealing scientifically with the real historical Jesus and not merely with the ahistorical, sacrificial Christ of dogma. The religious view of history promoted by this theology could not escape from the critical context of the general historical sciences, since it, too, was implicated in a personal, conditioned relationship to its object.[3]

In any case, whether one accepted or rejected God in this previous period, it was felt necessary to ground one's faith or one's disbelief in science—a procedure based upon the conviction that science was adequate to such purposes. As well as its affirmative attitude toward science, that earlier generation also proclaimed

B   *A positive relationship to the person of Jesus as answer to the question, What ought I to do?*

Just as in its religious art it preferred to place Jesus—even if in a somewhat idealized form—in a contemporary setting, the late nineteenth century also supposed that his ethic (apart from a few temporally conditioned elements which were judged to be accidental by-products) could be adapted readily to current circumstances. The appeal for ethical principles was not made simply, of course, to the Bible—such an appeal would have been considered rigid and anachronistic, excessively tied to the expectation of heavenly reward. One was supposed to construct his ethical system out of his own moral consciousness, or to deduce relevant maxims or commandments from the exigencies of his life situation. Thus, for example, Kant advanced the categorical imperative which willed the

[3] Ritschl and his school are typical representatives of this theology of experience and history. Also see the works of Wilhelm Herrmann.

highest good: its maxims would not permit the reduction of man to a means but rather recognized him as a rationally self-determined being. Or again, Marx called for class war to correct social injustices and thus sought to implement the intention of history.

As there was widespread feeling for the ethical grandeur of Jesus and a common understanding of his morality as Christian, so Jesus came to be seen as an ideal or model for ethical systems—whether idealist or Marxist in orientation. By the idealist he was esteemed as a leader who could guide man to his authentic humanity, who had died for his idea of man, and had thereby become immortal; for the Marxist he was seen to be the first revolutionary, battling for improved conditions on behalf of the poor and downtrodden against the priesthood and the bourgeoisie.

A somewhat different role was assigned to Jesus in the theological circle dominated by Luther's doctrine of justification, a school which could not join with ethical idealism because it was convinced that man's natural sinfulness necessitated an inner spiritual rebirth. The concepts of original sin and sin-unto-death were no longer understood in their classical sense, of course, and were reinterpreted in the light of the modern understanding of religious experience discussed above. According to this view, man only perceived his real quandary when he recognized that he was incapable of fulfilling the moral imperative with his own limited powers. Salvation meant that an individual must be freed from inner conflicts in order to become a whole person. Both judgment and redemption led man to the figure of Jesus in this theology, and in its preaching the ethical precept was intensified into the commandment of God. In his failure to meet this commandment, the sinner would experience the judgment of the sovereign God; but at the same time, he could encounter Jesus, who promised forgiveness and who had suffered death as a pledge of his loving kindness—the God of love who took upon himself the sins of men. What no ethical principle could accomplish, it was believed, would be fulfilled in this encounter between the sinner and the redeeming Jesus: a new life through the love of God.[4]

Despite their differences, these three positions—idealistic and Marxist ethics and the conception of rebirth through religious experience—had something in common: each in its distinctive fashion nominated itself as heir to the ethical teachings of Jesus. In response to the question, What ought I to do? they answered respectively, Jesus is ideal, leader, redeemer.

Another characteristic feature of the preceding era was to be found in

c   *The application of biblical conceptions to "faith in progress" in response to the question, What may I hope?*

As it touched upon the question, What may I hope? the conception of the kingdom of God assumed particular importance for this previous era. Rather than a miraculous, supernatural event which would break into this world from above and bring about its end, the kingdom was proclaimed as the ultimate aim of history, the goal toward which the natural evolution of man was pointing.

Through the ages, Christianity has variously reworked its understanding of the kingdom of God. One view has held it to be the heavenly reward which the godly might expect to obtain after faithfully traversing this earthly vale of woes. Or again, the Catholic Church has claimed this title in order to represent itself as an immediate participant in the eternal kingdom. The final twist, however, was left to that pair of fanatics—Hegel and Marx—who, with their prophecies of the world's end, marched further and further into the unknown until they arrived at a final conclusion for history. In short, they maintained that they themselves really belonged to those

[4] Wilhelm Herrmann, particularly, develops this view in his writings.

"last things" which their respective dogmatics claimed to depict in their final chapters. Thus idealism and Marxism also anticipated an end and fulfillment of history—but from their own distinctive perspectives and not, of course, in terms of the concept of the kingdom of God. Their hope did not extend to an afterlife, nor could their aspirations be contained within the sphere of religious institutions. Nor did they conceive of the end of history as some ultimate act in the drama of the cosmos, but rather as a current event, a development reaching out through all humanity—as a world principle unfolding in history. According to idealism, this world principle was the spirit or mind which develops in human culture and which humanity utilizes as its instrument and goal. For Marxism the principle was the natural necessity of man himself, whose fulfillment would be accomplished through the dictatorship of the proletariat which would guide the way to a classless paradise on earth. As in idealism the human spirit replaced the Holy Spirit, so in Marxism the suffering proletariat assumed the role of the Suffering Servant of God. The goal in both cases, if differently expressed, was the fulfillment of mankind—and thus each vision renewed the old dream of the golden age, the hope of seeing the kingdom of God finally realized on earth.

Similarly, the theology of the period, while its view of human nature was less optimistic, and though it certainly knew the kingdom to be of God's and not man's creation, could not restrain its enthusiasm for culture and its belief in progress. This theology confidently asserted God's role in world history and acclaimed cultural progress as the work of the divine kingdom. It viewed human history as a prefiguration of God's kingdom; it saw the church in its struggle for culture as a pioneer in a divinely ordained future.[5]

[5] This is close to Ritschl's definition: "The kingdom of God, then, is the correlate of God's love insofar as it is the association of men for reciprocal and common action from the motive of love—an association

Perhaps the most obvious disparity between the mood of our era and that of the nineteenth and early twentieth centuries is to be located in this characteristic hope for the future shared by idealism, Marxism and "cultural protestantism." But the dissimilarity in our respective attitudes towards science and towards Jesus is no less great. Certainly older notions have lingered on into the present. Proofs are still advanced for God, or one occasionally hears that faith in God and belief in science are incompatible. One still encounters the earlier images of Jesus as the true moral leader or as the religious hero. Nor has faith in the future entirely died out. On the whole, however, the old confidence in science, the religious quest for the historical Jesus, the optimistic hope for progress in our time—all must be acknowledged as essentially the characteristics of a bygone era. Our own epoch exhibits a quite different physiognomy; but before tracing its new features, let us ask

2   What has caused these alterations in the face of our time?

The reasons for our changed mood are not entirely novel, nor did they first appear in our generation; they had their fore-

which is determined, no longer by the natural conditions of affinity in the narrower sense, but by the unity of man's spiritual constitution." *The Christian Doctrine of Justification and Reconciliation,* trans. by H. R. Mackintosh and A. B. Macaulay (New York, Charles Scribner's Sons, 1900), p. 290.

runners in periods when quite different attitudes prevailed. Even while science reigned with absolute authority, some thinkers were pointing out the inherent limitations of scientific knowledge. We have already seen that Kant was the great "drawer of limits." Let us now consider certain other key qualifications which were neither affected by his *Critique* nor evident in the new systems that immediately followed his.

Writing in the middle of the last century, Feuerbach promulgated the theory that all so-called religious experience is really based in illusion, while Kierkegaard acclaimed a new dimension of reality beyond the immediate compass of science, which he designated "existence." [6]

There also come to mind scholars such as David Friedrich Strauss, who sketched a radical portrait of Jesus, a more alien and mythological portrait than even modern devotees of Jesus would accept as authentic.[7] By the beginning of our century, Albert Schweitzer had demolished the reigning conception of Jesus by casting suspicion upon the eschatological expectation, i.e. the faith in a Jesus who waits in attendance upon the last days.[8]

Even the cultural protestantism of the previous epoch was not so thoroughly optimistic in its faith in progress as it may have seemed. There were men like Schopenhauer, Eduard von Hartmann [9] and Nietzsche, or, among Swiss writers, the friends, Spitteler and Widmann—all of whom were burdened with profound pessimism regarding the creative possibilities of culture.[10]

[6] See Ludwig Feuerbach, *The Essence of Christianity* and Søren Kierkegaard, *Philosophical Fragments* and *Concluding Unscientific Postscript*.

[7] David Friedrich Strauss, *The Life of Jesus Critically Examined*.

[8] Albert Schweitzer, *The Quest of the Historical Jesus*, trans. by W. Montgomery, 3d ed. (London, A. & C. Black, 1954).

[9] Eduard von Hartmann, *Die Selbstzersetzung des Christentums und die Religion der Zukunft*.

[10] On Spitteler, see the author's work, *Prometheus und Christus* (1945).

In their day these men were outsiders, out of step with their own culture. But in our time their reservations have found potent echoes in recent movements and events. Today we witness

A *A crisis of confidence in science.*

People have been talking for some time about a general "crisis" in science: all sorts of obscurantists have exploited the problem of the validity of science's abstruse theories. Many of these criticisms have been exaggerated and taken much too seriously; for today we undeniably possess newly improved methods of investigation and as a result we have much more knowledge at our disposal in the form of dependable research findings—one need only mention atomic physics or psychoanalysis. Still it is true that the disproportionate claims made for the scientific method and its results by the previous generation have caused us to react with greater caution and reserve toward its powers. In the humane as well as the natural sciences, we all recognize that scientific knowledge, too, has its boundaries.

As a prime instance of such limits, contemporary philosophy now makes a distinction between the historiological (*historisch*) and the historical (*geschichtlich*). A judgment is scientifically historiological (*historischwissenschaftlich*) if it establishes, by analogy to the intellectual process, a matter of fact as objectively as possible on the basis of the best sources available and, further, if it classifies this fact in a comprehensive relationship to the world as known through previous investigation. Historicity (*Geschictlichkeit*), on the other hand, signifies an awareness of the fundamental limitations of all our statements and perceptions, and consequently of all results of research—an awareness based upon acknowledgment that our relative viewpoints are ultimately not objective. It is no longer likely that science will develop an absolutely valid world view which theology would have to challenge. Kant's battle against the construction of a rational metaphysics has not only been taken up again but actually extended.[11]

Or again, the unsettling of the world view of classical physics represents a shaking of the foundations of natural science comparable to that in historical research. Relativity and the quantum theory have undermined the absolute certainty of natural physical laws as well as the deterministic view of causality. This is not to say that we can no longer use such laws in our calculations, but they now are stripped of their absolute character and employed merely as statistical rules of order. This discernment has had radical consequences for metaphysical speculation in particular; it prohibits, for instance, the construction of a definitive scientific view of reality on the basis of which one might contest faith in God simply on the grounds that he cannot be detected or demonstrated in human experience. Natural science today is actually on the way to religion.[12]

But if Christian faith concludes on the basis of this fundamental shift in scientific understanding that there is a special mode of religious experience which can be supported scientifically, its apologetic must deal with the objection connected with the name of Feuerbach, i.e. the notion that "special" religious experience presupposes man's yearning after salvation, that it implies a projection of unfulfilled human desires into the heavenly sphere—in short, that religious experience is an illusion. As a result of Nietzsche's critique and Marx's slogan, "Religion is the opiate of the masses," and because of the thorough psychologizing of modern thought, the suspicion that religion is, indeed, only an illusion has gained considerable headway in the general consciousness. We are faced today with widespread scepticism regarding so-called

[11] Karl Jaspers, "Geschichtlichkeit," in *Philosophie*, II (Berlin, Springen-Verlag, 1948), pp. 397 ff.
[12] See Bernhard Bavink, *Die Naturwissenschaft auf dem Wege zur Religion* (Basel, T. Moraus Verlag, 1943).

religious experience—a scepticism which is not entirely unjustified.

To the loss of faith in science there corresponds

B   *A fundamental modification of our view of the personality of Jesus.*

In its early stages, historical research replaced the traditional doctrine of the divine-human Redeemer with the notion—developed from source study—of Jesus as a real, human personality. The latter figure was a Jesus who certainly lived and thought to a great extent within the characteristic forms of his time, but who also projected eternal religious and moral values, which he himself embodied, beyond the limited span of his own immediate epoch. It seemed a fairly simple process to separate this kernel of value from its shell and thus to achieve a direct relation to his timeless vision.[13]

As historical research progressed, however, and especially as it penetrated more deeply into the available religious-historical materials, it was discovered that to distinguish the kernel of Jesus' essential nature from its shell was not such a simple task after all. Contrary to the original assumption that Jesus could be isolated from his environment, he was found to be inextricably bound to it: it was seen that his teachings and acts, his suffering and death, as well as the proclamation connected with these events by primitive Christianity, could only be understood in terms of their original context. Furthermore, what historical research had hoped to cast aside as mere extrinsic historical raiment proved to be the primary concern of Jesus and his Gospel; at the same time, the so-called "eternal significance" was unfrocked as mere modern elaboration and innovation.

On reevaluation, the real Jesus turns out to have been a powerful historical personality, but a personality who lived and

[13] Perhaps the best known example of this viewpoint is Adolf V. Harnack's *What is Christianity?* (New York, Harper & Row, 1957).

acted in an intellectual environment almost entirely foreign and incomprehensible to modern man. Today this primitive *Weltanschauung* is shared by only a few obscure religious sects, or reserved in dogmatics for that short final chapter devoted to the doctrine of eschatology or "last things." This more recently discovered Jesus lived fully in the eschatology of his time; he shared its expectation of the imminent coming of the kingdom of God, the supernatural consummation of the world in a cosmic upheaval transforming heaven and earth. The distinctive feature in Jesus' own understanding of these last events is now seen to consist in the fact that he nominated himself as the central actor in this cosmic drama. In line with the late apocalyptic expectation of the Jewish scribes—the imminent end of the world and the actual irruption of God's kingdom into contemporary events—Jesus believed himself appointed by God to the role of future Messiah, "coming on the clouds of heaven with power and great glory." Only in this mythological context can the words and deeds of Jesus be explained adequately. His ethical commands are no longer interpreted as dealing with the necessities of this passing world, but rather as serving—in the short period remaining before the end—to prepare the kingdom of the elect. He goes to his death in order to reappear as Messiah, to bring about the end of the world, and to prepare the kingdom of God. As is this kingdom itself, so is the Holy Spirit which he promises to his followers also an entirely supernatural power.[14]

What can idealism with its gospel of the human spirit, or Marxism with its social striving directed toward the current scene, or religious experience, or cultural protestantism, possibly make of this radically foreign eschatological Jesus? How can we still hold out hope for some viable answer to the question, What ought I to do? when faced with this conception

[14] See Fritz Buri, *Die Bedeutung der neutestamentlichen Eschatologie für die neuere protestantische Theologie* (Zurich und Leipzig, M. Niehaus, 1935).

of the imminent destruction of our world? At first representing only the hypothetical result of scientific research, this absolutely foreign conceptual climate of the eschatological Jesus suddenly and unexpectedly found its way into the general consciousness of our time.

What made this development possible was

c   *The collapse of modern "faith in progress" in the cultural crisis of our time.*

Faith in progress had already been dealt a severe blow by World War I. Almost momentarily, cultural optimism disappeared to be replaced by bleak pessimism, high-flown plans and hopes were scrapped, and we entered an era of hopelessness and scepticism—a general mood made only more stark by the catastrophic developments of subsequent years. Today we hardly know whether to laugh or weep at the naïveté of the pre-World War I optimists, but in any case we no longer have any desire to participate in their attitude towards the world and towards human nature; their hope of the kingdom of God is alien to us.

The revolution in our philosophy of history is dramatically represented by the work of Oswald Spengler, the title of which, *The Decline of the West,* has become a byword of our time. Today even Marxism no longer places its confidence solely in class-war ideology, but is turning to new methods and appealing to new forces. Cultural protestantism has given way to a "crisis theology" which no longer understands the kingdom of God as the culmination of social evolution but rather adopts an eschatological judgment which stands over and against all human strivings, and thus it, too, has been responsive to the emergent spiritual temper of our time.[15]

For if the concepts of judgment and end are again current,

[15] The strongest expression of this change is represented by Karl Barth's *The Epistle to the Romans,* trans. by Edwyn C. Hoskyns (New York, Oxford University Press, 1953), as it compares with what he writes in his *Church Dogmatics,* II,1 (Edinburgh, T. & T. Clark, 1936–62), pp. 635 ff.

and if we again see history from the perspective of the "last days," it is not primarily because of devotional or scholarly concerns derived from the Bible but rather because our own time has now taken on an apocalyptic cast. We have experienced disappointment and failure and can see no sure way out of our dilemma, and such a climate is ideal for the imagery of the eschatological expectation of the "last times." We have witnessed destruction and bestiality which make us doubt that history has meaning or man, goodness; the apocalyptic archetypes of the beast from the underworld and the final conflagration have been reawakened in us. Atomic physicists speak of the possible annihilation of our planet. For our generation, faith in progress has fallen into the "slough of despond," and out of this the apocalypse has again erupted into the general consciousness. In immediate response to current events, many are again reading the Bible "with that familiar sense of the eschatological." [16]

With the three features of our age indicated above—the upheavals within science, the renewed discovery of biblical eschatology, the collapse of faith in progress—there have emerged

3 Two typical expressions of the face of our time.

We can represent these two expressions in terms of the three aspects of the age to which we have drawn special attention

[16] Paul Althaus, *Die letzten Dinge*, 6th ed. (Gutersloh, Carl Bertelsmann, 1956).

above. Let us examine their respective answers to our central questions, What can I know? What ought I to do? What may I hope?

In answer to the question, What can I know? against the background of the crisis of confidence in science, there stand in contrast

A   *Atheism and revelation faith.*

These two representative exponents of our time have been produced in equal measure by the radical change in our estimation of man's capacity for knowledge—a radical change due largely to events that intervened between our immediate predecessors and ourselves.

Let us first examine the pattern of atheism. Present-day atheism differs from its forebears in that earlier versions took the negative part in a contest in which one side sought to prove God scientifically while the other employed science as an argument against his existence. This debate format was relatively orderly: proof could be measured against proof.

Today, as science once again acknowledges its incompetence to deal with this sphere of human concern, a mutual context of proof leveled for or against God no longer exists. Instead we hear: "One cannot speak scientifically about God; can one speak at all today about God? Can any certainty whatsoever be guaranteed in such an enterprise? The individual, perhaps, may occasionally feel that he has won some measure of certainty; but is he ever really in any position to offer a convincing account of the basis of his own faith, let alone that of others? Religion is a private affair, a luxury article, or a means of reassurance—a highly precarious kind of reassurance, however, subject to dangerous errors and machinations. One does best not to meddle with it: in the last analysis, one can get along comfortably without such a system."

This is the mode of argumentation as well as the effect of present-day atheism, which proclaims with Nietzsche, "God is dead." [17] As long as one had to prove that there was no God, one was still contending with at least the possibility of his existence. Present-day atheism takes a much more radical stance: the question of God's existence, it suggests, is no longer a live issue.

At the other extreme, however, a much more radical faith in revelation has been developed than was current, for example, in the theology of religious experience around the turn of the century. The latter theology did acknowledge revelation, but with its stress on the experiential phenomena emergent in history, it more distinctively laid claim to the historical personality of Jesus as the basis for a scientifically shaped mode of faith. It went so far as to suggest that it could independently verify, and thus guarantee with scientific assurance, this historical faith.

With the advent of the crisis of confidence in science, however, the old suspicion that religion is illusory was voiced again —but now to be sounded even by theology itself. It was acknowledged that historical judgments can never be considered absolutely valid but instead remain hypotheses. For this reason, it was maintained, history is much too unsound a basis for faith. Particularly, it was noted that if one argues human need as the criterion of religious truth, one runs straight into the arms of Feuerbach—who had long before asserted that religion is essentially nothing else than an illusory longing for tranquility.[18]

Further, theologians now declared that faith has nothing to do with science and that faith betrays itself whenever it endeavors to verify itself scientifically. "Faith is based in revelation. Revelation, moreover, is not a psychologically demonstrable or controllable experience. Nor is it a power to be grasped by historical methods—neither by the so-called his-

[17] Nietzsche, *The Joyful Wisdon*, no. 125; compare Martin Heidegger's "Nietzsches Wort, 'Gott ist Tot' " in *Holzwege*, p. 125.
[18] Karl Barth, *Church Dogmatics*, II, 1, p. 292.

torical Jesus nor the God immanent in world history. It is rather a vertical happening from on high: the Word of God become flesh in Jesus Christ. It is this Word and nothing else that matters. Only in the Christ does God reveal himself, and beyond this 'event' there can be only worship of idols." [19] Thus we are exhorted by present-day revelation theology.

A similar antithesis is apparent in our current intellectual situation with regard to the ethical question, What ought I to do? This set of contrasting theses is embodied in

B *Nihilism and redemption through Christ.*

In light of the eschatological figure of Jesus and his eschatological expectation of the kingdom of God, we have already asked, What ought modern man to do? Neither a basis for reality nor a norm for ethics can be derived from this mythology. We can at best appreciate it as an interesting, yet quite foreign, chapter in religious history. How can modern man bridge the distance between that time and his own place of understanding? Hasn't history confuted the eschatological expectation? Would an adherence to this primitive understanding of history not be totally inadequate to the necessities of our own time, indeed, cause more harm than any possible benefit? Can one use the Sermon on the Mount to formulate a national policy? Would not all order be placed in jeopardy by using it for such contemporary purposes?

It is because of such difficulties that the eschatological understanding of early Christianity has been so variously reworked and reinterpreted in the course of history—the most recent version being the idealistic Gospel of humanitarian and of cultural protestantism. However, by what authority do such differing formulations appoint themselves as exponents of the true Christianity, the true religion, the true ethic? Are they not, together with all other extrinsic Christian systems, only

[19] Karl Barth, *Church Dogmatics*, I,2, "The Revelation of God as the Abolition of Religion," pp. 280 ff.

external schema that man has seized upon in an effort to order his life and world—schema to which, however, no absolute, eternal allegiance is due, and which are useful only in so far as they permit the intellect to come to grips with its own time? "The true ring has probably been lost"—but our situation is even worse than in Lessing's time for he at least lived securely with his faith: in his humanistic religion, the "true ring" had been rediscovered. But today one is confronted with inherently diverse rings each man selects or makes for himself, and we can no longer hope to discover the one true ring amidst such a curious welter of viewpoints.

How readily this situation can lead to the conclusion that all ethical systems are relative, that there is no ethical truth, that good and evil are relative concepts, that man may do anything—for everything is permitted from one viewpoint or another.

The nihilism of our day has actually drawn this conclusion. It is a most desperate conclusion, for it not only destroys all sense of community but also places the individual personality in jeopardy. In order to find a way out of his dilemma—even at the risk of losing himself—the nihilist chooses to affirm that he is in fact caught in a hopeless situation. He is prepared to take this situation upon himself, even if his decision means that he must share its tragic doom. Only with the defiant courage to embrace nothingness, he believes, can he give meaning to his existence.[20]

It is precisely this stubborn self-assertion—even in the face of failure—that is criticized by Christian redemptive faith as the offspring of human sin and depravity; it sees nihilism as the ultimate consequence of any way of life without Christ. Man,

[20] For instance, Heidegger speaks of "running towards" or "anticipation of death" (*Vorlaufens in den Tod*) in *Being and Time*, trans. by John Macquarrie and Edward Robinson (New York, Harper & Row, 1962), pp. 262 ff., and elsewhere of "being-constrained-in-nothing" (*Hineingehaltenseins ins Nichts*).

it preaches, cannot escape this path if he pursues his life without a faith framed and conceived in response to the redemption accomplished by Jesus' death and resurrection: natural man is totally lost. Further, redemptive theology attributes this sinful alienation not only to those who would appeal to the worthiness of man but also to those who quest for a premature religious experience, i.e. those who understand redemption as the psychological experience of the divine love of God in the person of Jesus. The breakdown of humanistic thought in our time and the human frailty which always thrusts itself to the fore in the "Jesus-experience," are interpreted as apparent proofs of the sinfulness of religious experience as a means of redemption—since this path to redemption would bypass the cross and the empty grave in its progress from the virgin birth to the ascension of Christ.

Redemptive theology not only believes that it can restore the original sense of the biblical account of redemption by means of its dogma of the saving work of the God-man, but is also led by its interpretation of redemption to claim that the only legitimate well-being for the individual or for mankind is to be discovered in these witnessed events and in a pious acceptance of them.

To the question, What ought I to do? redemptive theology gives the answer, Believe in the saving work of God in Christ, for it is to be understood as having been accomplished in our behalf. What man does is not important, but rather what God has done. Man remains a sinner, but in Christ, God is merciful to him. This belief must be firmly maintained—unbroken in all our brokenness.[21]

Now let us direct our attention to the hope of our time with regard to history. From what has been recounted above, it is not surprising that we discover another irreconcilable polarity, namely

[21] Karl Barth, *Church Dogmatics*, I,2, p. 331.

c *Naturalistic despair over history and the proclamation of supernatural redemptive history.*

Since the catastrophic events of our era have seriously undermined idealistic and even Marxist ideology, historical interpretation in the West appears to be in desperate straits. What can we expect from future history? Will there even be a future? Is there, for that matter, even a history to be distinguished from mere natural occurrence? Is history anything but an extension of the struggle for existence, elaborated by weapons of the inventive human mind as it designs its own destruction, but nevertheless bound within the sphere of nature? Do not the so-called ideas of the spirit merely serve the natural drive for power which, while it may transcend individual self-assertion, bears within itself the seeds of incomprehensible destructiveness? Is history anything but the *fable convenue* of the victor? Is man anything but a "monstrously insane, rapacious, species of ape"? [22]

Darwin explained the evolution of man and his history according to the natural principle of survival of the fittest. Nietzsche adapted this view of man to the interpretation of history through his doctrines of "the will to power" and the training of the "superman"—a training for the conquest of "the eternal recurrence." With the collapse of faith in progress, this naturalistic interpretation of history and culture has prevailed. Spengler's organic theory of culture is one of its derivatives; he conceived of cultures as organisms which evolve from youth to maturity, then senescence and finally death—with all the necessity and irreversibility of a natural process. He excluded the possibility of cultural renewal, for according to its intrinsic law of development, a culture passes through its various stages until eventually, when its destiny is fulfilled, it is obliterated; a culture is completely ruled by its natural

[22] See Theodor Lessing, *Geschichte als Sinngebung des Sinnlosen,* 3d ed. (1922).

destiny. Our generation has witnessed the ultimate abortion of such naturalism in the racial theory of National Socialism. Its catastrophic effects can surely never be surpassed, and today, following its suppression, we can only ask, what next can possibly fill the vacuum in the German historical consciousness.

Perhaps it will be the interpretation of history which has developed in response to the Nazi era and to the rediscovery of the biblical expectation of the "last days" in current Protestant theology. Initially, the new understanding of the kingdom of God as a power breaking in upon history through God's act was connected to the theories of social reform in early Marxism.[23] But such "religious socialism," closely related, then as always, to cultural protestantism, was soon superseded by crisis theology in which the kingdom of God was understood as the perpetual "No" to all forms of human striving: "If today one notes where nihilism leads, and at the same time cannot dismiss the fact that the New Testament mentions not only the proximity of the kingdom of God transcending time, but also its coming in history—if also its annihilation of history—then instead of just a crisis of history one must also speak of God's redemptive plan for history." Thus, once again today we have a redemptive theology that endeavors to understand history in terms of the creation, the fall of man, the old and new covenants, the redeeming work of Christ, and the completion of history in Christ's second coming. According to this conception, we live in the time between the ascension and the second coming: in the cross and the resurrection of the Christ, the powers of this world have been decisively conquered; Christ sits in authority, and what we now experience is only the rearguard, delaying action of the defeated demons; against them our Christian commitment enjoins us to raise on high

[23] Above all by Leonhard Ragaz.

the signs of our belief in the coming of our Lord, upon whose appearance all salvation depends. . . .[24]

This is very comforting mythology, but since it is only mythology, it is a feeble solace in no way adequate to fill the vacuum which has resulted from the collapse of confidence in culture and from the catastrophe of naturalism.

It has been incumbent upon us to examine the principal features of the face of our time, as well as those of the earlier period against which it stands in significant contrast. But there remains a further task—and one which will be difficult to accomplish without giving offense—namely, to unveil

4 The anomalous feature in the face of our time.

This anomalous feature is not simply the manifestation of discord between opposed tendencies which we have just traced along various lines. Such discord in itself would not necessarily be a liability; it could even be considered a promising sign of an inner struggle towards new goals and accomplishments. The really ominous factor in our current intellectual climate is that despite their differences, the points of view whose areas of conflict have been analyzed above betray one fatal area of agreement. This agreement consists in a thoroughly negative

[24] An exponent of this contemporary theology of redemptive history is Oscar Cullmann, *Christ and Time*, trans. by Floyd V. Filson (London, SCM Press, 1951).

and destructive attitude towards human capabilities—an attitude which is all the worse since it precludes the very meaning
which Christian faith could have for our age.

In this destructive anti-Christianity lies the dangerous threat
posed by contemporary philosophy and theology—a threat that
must be recognized before it can be met.

Atheism and revelation theology are united in that they cannot apprehend the God-man, and in that they offer no understanding of God apart from a special form of supernatural
revelation in the Christ which atheism denies and revelation
theology cannot vindicate. We must ask these two conflicting
systems, these alleged modes of thinking and believing, of
reason and faith, what has happened to the biblical concept
of the creator, the understanding expressed, for example, by
Paul: "Ever since the creation of the world his invisible nature,
namely, his eternal power and deity, has been clearly perceived
in the things that have been made" (Rom. 1:20).

Further, both nihilism and faith in redemption through
Christ assert that man can neither know nor do the good: both
see man as tragically lost. The nihilist is prepared to take this
tragedy upon himself, the religious believer lets Christ bear it.
From neither of these perspectives does one achieve the New
Being; the nihilist remains a doubter and the Christian, a sinner. What kind of redeeming reality does Christ signify for
Paul when the latter declares, "If any one is in Christ, he is a
new creation; the old has passed away, behold, the new has
come" (II Cor. 5:17)?

Finally, neither naturalism nor the theology of redemptive
history has been able to give positive meaning to history. The
former surrenders history to nature and consequently denies its
very substance; the latter interprets history as the domain of
the devil and consoles itself with an illusory, "miraculous"
story. How very far each has progressed from what Jesus intended with his tidings of the kingdom of God: "Repent for
the kingdom of heaven is at hand" (Matt. 4:14).

Thus we read the face of our time as requiring the most cogent answers to the three questions:

How can we speak of God?
What does Christ mean to us?
What is the meaning of history and of the kingdom of God?

To answer these questions and to indicate what Christian faith might be in our time is not an easy task, for we can know nothing apart from our limited historical context. The face of our time is also our face, and ours must be a faith appropriate to our era if we are to see its possibilities and respond to its claims. It is our face that must be remade by faith, our face that must be stamped afresh with a new inner being.

This is a difficult venture and not without danger, but neither is it without promise; for, to conclude with Hölderlin:

> God though near
> Eludes our grasp.
> But danger wakes
> His saving power.
> —"Patmos"

Two

HOW CAN WE SPEAK

OF GOD?

✝

Directed by Kant's three questions, What can I know? What ought I to do? What may I hope? the first chapter attempted to sketch a portrait of our time. The face which emerged was mutilated, terribly torn by the radical opposition of atheism and belief in revelation, of nihilism and redemption in Christ, of naturalism and supernatural redemptive history. But it was not the mutual exclusiveness of these extremes alone that startled us. We were confronted by the much more shocking fact that in one significant respect, despite all their differences, these positions demonstate full agreement, namely, in a negative, destructive attitude towards man's capacities for knowledge, towards man's actions and towards human history. We discovered a type of faith in revelation which, in regard to man's knowledge of God, is no less negatively disposed than philosophical atheism. We saw nihilism and Christian redemptive faith united against every positive assessment of the moral capacities of man. We found the substance of history as the sphere of culture sacrificed equally by the redemptive and naturalistic views of history. What, we must ask, has happened to the notion of a creator God, the actuality of a redemptive Christ, the realization of the kingdom of God? Surely each of these conceptions belongs within the Christian faith. Thus, from our analysis of the philosophy and theology of the contemporary scene, three pressing problems emerge: How are we to speak of God? What does Christ mean for us? What is the status of history and of the kingdom of God? The present

47

chapter attacks the first of these problems, How can we speak of God?

From the preceding exposition it ought to be clear that we can no longer speak of God with the self-assurance of earlier eras. The objections raised by contemporary atheism as well as by present-day revelation theology against man's capacity to speak of God must be taken into account. If we deceive ourselves on this point and continue to speak of God as we did in the past and as we might still prefer to speak now, we shall divorce ourselves from our own time and can not be surprised if we are misunderstood or even ignored. A living Christian faith must be the faith of its own particular time—otherwise it should be relegated to some museum.[1]

This does not mean that we should try to prescribe any particular form for the spiritual and intellectual climate of our own time. Quite the contrary; as children of our age we must listen to its distinctive voice, not in bondage to some fashionable movement but rather with a liberating awareness of ourselves as men caught up in its sway. To this end, an investigation of the conflicts between atheism and faith in revelation (as well as their fatal areas of agreement, which have been pointed out) may well be of some immediate use.

In the process of exposing the false consequences of these contemporary movements as well as their justifiable concerns, there may hopefully be discovered some way in which we may speak authentically of God. In this endeavor, however, special care must be taken lest what is said about God in this limited context in any way be misunderstood as the last or definitive word on the subject. Major objections could rightfully be raised against any such claim. The very nature of the question, What can we know? precludes the possibility of speaking adequately of God, even on the basis of the renewed signif-

[1] Karl Jaspers also urges a reprieve from such a "museum-like existence" through a "metamorphosis of biblical religion" in *The European Spirit* (London, SCM Press, 1948).

icance of the Christ, which we shall attempt to develop in a later chapter. Yet this study does have its own grounds for undertaking some initial approaches to the problem. The present chapter outlines these approaches in part, and begins by noting

1   The legitimate concerns of atheism and faith in revelation.

Legitimate concerns must be recognized on either side of the boundaries of faith. Neither atheism nor revelation faith could have achieved such a prominent place in the current scene if it did not express fundamental truths. One would be distorting the full significance of these forces to recognize only their destructive impulses, their obvious inadequacies. Neither can be rejected out of hand as mere scepticism or mere superstition. Men of profound intelligence and faith confront us in these movements: the honesty and import of our attempt to speak of God will only be served by our willingness to listen impartially to their critical voices and to take their concerns seriously. Therefore, let us investigate

A   *The theological significance of atheism.*

Atheism, as its name implies, is the antithesis of faith in God. The atheist chooses to repudiate rather than believe in God, yet in this repudiation he continues to involve himself with God. His position is not autonomous but depends upon the reality that he denies. If there were no faith in God there could be no

God to be rejected; for only where assertions are being made about God can these assertions also be disputed—the positive statement precedes the negative denial. Atheism shadows theology along all its paths, pursues it into its haunts: metamorphoses in theology alter the very substance of atheism itself. The assertions of atheism—while patently in negative form—are always oriented towards and based upon the postulates and positive assertions of theology. The fervor of the atheist is no less than that of the beliver, and in this regard Nietzsche has his Zarathustra admit that he himself is transformed along with the priests whom he scorns.[2] Against its will, atheism is theology—negative theology to be sure, but even in its denial, still theology.

Atheism always directs its attack against a particular theology or a particular conception of God, against a specific mode of knowledge used by faith in experiencing, delineating and defending its conception of God, and, above all, against the claim to absolute validity that theology attaches to its own views—its apparent disregard of their idiosyncratic character.

It is precisely against these idiosyncrasies, which it sees as belonging to the very essence of theology, that atheism levies its criticism; it refuses to yield to any conception of God in which it discovers all too human traits, a God who—in the mirror of the creation of man recounted in the Bible—is fashioned after man's own image. The atheist also repudiates such a God because he cannot locate him in the world of his alleged creation—a real world which seems to exclude the kind of God described by theology. The atheist is dissatisfied with the notion of a world above and beyond the natural sphere. It seems to him too much the product of man's furtive desires, the consequence of his unfulfilled longings, a refuge for human weakness.

Atheism, moreover, does not trust the methods by which

2 "The Priests" in *Thus Spake Zarathustra.*

theology thinks itself capable of securing its conception of God in the face of sceptical doubts and questionings. Why, the atheist asks, should one renounce the application of reason to theological matters when reason is clearly the instrument of knowledge in other areas, and when reason was presumably granted to man by the creator—if such a creator exists? Lurking behind the theory that man must bow down and blindly obey is there not to be discovered, the atheist asks, the lust for power of a priesthood which seeks to subjugate the masses? Does not the clergy, for this very reason, hope to destroy man's confidence in his capacity to know so as to make him tractable to the imposition of whatever dogmas it may wish to supply? And aren't those who complacently accept this bondage to religious faith simply weak-minded, vacillating individuals?

If one merely replies by confronting the atheist with the demands of God's Word without a willingness to engage him in discussion about related issues, he will point out that this Word always appears to him in the mouths of men and that even in the Bible it assumes the limitations of its human spokesmen. It will be quite natural for the atheist to point to the relativity of the evidence supporting God's Word and thus to question the authority of its claims. The challenge that he base his life on this uncertain manifestation of the Word is exactly what the atheist repudiates, not because he lacks the courage to resolve to do so but because he wants to conserve his courage for real mysteries, not those whose origins seem all too apparent.

All in all, atheism cannot simply be reproached for stubborn godlessness, evil and arrogance. On the contrary, the atheist may crave belief. He may have struggled more with his decision to reject God than many a believer who travels the broad way of a traditional faith out of mere indolence or weakness— indeed, who is driven to religious fanaticism because atheism has threatened his complacency and stirred his anxieties.

Admittedly the atheist can also become a destructive fanatic, sometimes because he is still infected by traces of the faith which he despises or because he is enraged by the lies, the arrogance, the false pride in the guise of humility that he discovers in so much of what passes for man's response to God. But for all his nay-saying, the atheist may really want to say "Yes"—an honest "Yes," however, a "Yes" to God and not to a false idol, and in the face of such idolatry he becomes a temple stormer. Yet even if, as is the case with the modern atheist, he has left such disputes behind and is contented with a godless world, one still perceives in his statements the will for unconditional honesty and thus implicitly an ultimate respect for silence regarding the inexpressible.

And by this response, atheism makes an indispensable contribution to theology. Its critique is the necessary corrective to all our discourse concerning God—without its close attention, our words stand in constant danger of becoming mere godless babble. This, in the truest sense, is the theological significance of atheism.[3]

Next, we must not overlook

B   *The concerns of revelation theology in its current radical*
   form.

In bare outline, revelation theology's train of thought—at least on its negative side—seems to be identical with the arguments of atheism recounted above. And in revelation theology we are also confronted by a faith which in common with all other faiths—certainly at its inception and still in part today—manifests an all too human confidence in itself.

Such a faith would not be a creation of our own time if it were merely the homely piety and stubborn orthodoxy of the last century, that is, if its dialectic could readily be reconverted into those antiquated forms. But through its major proponents

---

[3] The theological significance of atheism is also stressed by Paul Tillich. See, for instance, "The Two Types of Philosophy of Religion," in *Theology of Culture* (New York, Oxford University Press, 1959).

it exhibits a startlingly modern face. It places great confidence in contemporary man and his philosophy—often greater confidence than more ostensibly progressive theologies. How else, if it were not born out of the crisis of our time, could it have won such a measure of success in our generation?

This theology is not only aware of critical text analysis but also of the crisis in scientific doctrines. Above all, it has adopted Feuerbach's theory of religion as its own. Appealing to Calvin's doctrines regarding the human intellect, the perpetual factory of idols, revelation theology has made it its business to unmask religion as the product of human illusions.[4]

Revelation, to the contrary, is understood by this theology as something entirely "other," as an event independent of all human modes of knowledge, as an irruption from God's world into our own. For this reason revelation can be neither engendered nor verified by man; it stands uniquely under God's control. The Word of God is an event; where it shall be promulgated and believed is also the working of God. With the word of man as its vehicle, however, revelation becomes something other than God's Word: thus, its relation to man is as the manna in the wilderness which the Israelites could not preserve but always received in new measure. The essence of faith cannot be grasped psychologically, for this would lead to a purely human God. Perhaps, revelation theology suggests, the proper image to use in speaking of God is that of the wheel, the spokes of which all point to a center. In order that the wheel be used, however, this center must remain empty. For this reason, faith—as it is humanly apprehended—is a "void."[5]

Until recently the opposition of God's Word and man's word, in which the essence of the biblical command was discovered, could be expressed in philosophical categories: God was the

[4] Karl Barth, "Religion as Unbelief," *Church Dogmatics*, I,2, pp. 297 ff.
[5] These are all well-known images and concepts from the period of Karl Barth's *The Epistle to the Romans*.

unconditioned who manifested himself only in our thoroughly conditioned statements. But now this concept of the (masculine *der*) unconditioned has become something other than the (neuter *das*) unconditioned of philosophical speculation. The unconditioned has come to be viewed as an illicit analogy for expressing the relation between God and man, and consequently, the schism has widened between theological and philosophical thought. If revelation theology once considered the biblical mythology to be an adequate expression for the dialectic between God and man across the unbridgeable gulf dividing them, it has in time come to disregard completely the philosophical dialectic. From the perspective of revelation, philosophical analysis seems to be only one more attempt on the part of man to speak of God out of himself.[6] Thus, only mythology survives, i.e. God's speaking and his manifestation in the natural world are now seen as belonging entirely to the substance of myth rather than to the history of God in space and time.[7]

This mythological faith, which excludes all rational criteria, raises many difficulties that demand examination. Nevertheless, in a time when it is widely assumed that all mythology must submit to exposure by science as the product of mere fantasy or lingering superstition, revelation theology must be given credit for holding fast to the mythological account of the world and for refusing to let our awareness of this significant mythology fade. It therefore impedes the terrible and substantial loss which has increasingly threatened the Western

[6] This attitude reflects the distinction between Karl Barth's projected outline of the *Christian Dogmatics* (1927) and his later *Church Dogmatics*. Compare this to his *Nein*, first published in 1934, translated as *No* (London, The Century Press, 1946); to Emil Brunner, and to his own theological past.

[7] In this connection see Rudolf Bultmann's *"Neues Testament und Mythologie"* in *Kerygma und Mythos*, edited by H. W. Bartsch, 2d ed. (1951). Translated by Reginald H. Fuller as *Kerygma and Myth* (London, S.P.C.K., 1953).

intellect since the Enlightenment. It has preserved for us the very real world of biblical symbolism.[8]

How could we speak of God without this biblical tradition and its forms of expression—symbols without which it would be scarcely possible to conceive of God and certainly inefficacious to proclaim him to our society? Even if the preservation of this irreplaceable store of symbols is not the chief issue at stake for this theology, its firm adherence to the Bible is still a fact of greatest positive significance—especially in a time when the German "racial soul" would otherwise spawn out of its own abyss its "myth of the twentieth century" and substitute it for the symbolism of the Bible.

Yet in spite of the positive significance which faith in revelation has for the attempt to speak of God in our day, and before its practical consequences are examined, attention must be directed to

2 The false consequences of contemporary atheism and revelation theology.

In each instance, false consequences derive from an attempt to absolutize things which cannot be absolutized—by the former, reason, and by the latter, faith at the expense of reason.

[8] A factor which Karl Jaspers continues to stress, and in which his estimation of the Bible is grounded. Compare "For the Biblical Religion," in *The Perennial Scope of Philosophy*, trans. by Ralph Manheim (New York, Philosophical Library, 1949), pp. 97 ff.

A   *The self-absolutization of atheism.*

Atheism's war against idols is undeniably justified. Philosophy or theology fails to recognize its own limitations if it pretends that it can speak adequately about God in human terminology. Our speculations can never encompass being-in-itself or being-as-a-whole, but rather treat only particular beings as they seem to us. Similarly, the Word of God, even when spoken by men of faith, is still only the human word. In faith we merely express human conceptions of God, and we dare not exchange such notions for God himself.

But along with its justified protest against an all too human interpretation of God, atheism, for its part, violates its own logic if it concludes that there is in truth no God, and that all discussion of God is simply public superstition. By such an assertion, atheism delivers itself into the camp of the superstitious. Certainly our conceptual knowledge can only be applied to presently existing objects and clearly God does not permit himself to be dealt with as such a presence—to do so would be to make himself an idol! Moreover, when atheism asserts that there can be no God because his existence cannot be proved, surely it is absolutizing its own confidence in the finite sphere of human perception—as if our thinking could determine what really exists, as if only what we perceive really exists, or as if reason comprehends the whole of reality and is not rather only one aspect of what is manifest within it.[9] Surely reason is something other than the things which it apprehends; and surely this restriction makes reason neither infinite nor absolute, but rather limited and finite in the ex-

[9] In this context, Karl Jaspers' concept of the "Comprehensive" (*Umgreifenden*) is perhaps relevant. See his detailed accounts in *Von der Wahrheit* (München, R. Piper, 1947), translated in part as *Truth and Symbol* with introduction by J. Wilde, W. Kilaback and W. Kimmel (New York, Twayne Publishers, 1959), or in *Einführung in die Philosophie* (Zürich, Artemis-Verlag, 1950).

treme. It is this restriction, however, which atheism overlooks. In its struggle against theological absolutes, it absolutizes its philosophy and, itself, becomes superstitious.[10]

Now to be accurate, it must be acknowledged that there is an atheism today which is careful to restrict its positive statements. It is content to bypass the critique of philosophical and theological mythologies in order to get on with its own daily agenda, i.e. it can be satisfied with the finite world and its objects—even if this world is godless. Yet even this ostensible process of suspending and thus dispensing with the question of God is a decision—and, to be sure, a negative one. If, in fact, there is a God, one cannot just suspend one's judgment about him—anymore than if he did not exist—for clearly one is still making a decision either for or against him. One can give either a "Yes" or "No" and cannot evade the question.[11]

Even the pantheistic form of atheism which one encounters occasionally is to be rejected as inconsistent. It maintains the view that this world is all there is, that what we perceive *is* the world so far as we can know it, and that to postulate a world beyond this one, in whose context God might be located, would be a contradiction in terms. Nevertheless, the relation of our known world to that which endures independently of (and beyond) our perceptions remains to be considered, i.e. the pantheists must clarify whether they are making a superficial or a fundamental distinction, and how, if God is understood as being at one with the world, it is possible to distinguish the world on the one hand and God on the other. In any case, all particular beings, and among them man, would have to be understood as some form of the manifestation of the all-one,

[10] See Karl Jaspers, *The Perennial Scope of Philosophy*, pp. 118 ff.

[11] For his part, Heidegger wants to leave the question open (see, for example, his *Vom Wesen des Grundes*, 1929, p. 98); while Jean Paul Sartre responds with a radical "No," most forcefully illustrated in his play *The Flies*.

God-world.[12] This conception—as we shall see in a later connection—not only leads to impossible ethical consequences but also stands in opposition to our understanding of the world, an understanding which does not allow us any closed system of being. Further, it contradicts our awareness of our own limitations—for it is not as gods (in the sense of the biblical conception of the creator) that we gain consciousness of ourselves but rather as creatures. However, before we continue our positive exposition we must criticize

B *The inconsistencies of revelation theology.*

We have stressed the value of this form of Christian faith for our time. It preserves the biblical symbols from premature abandonment or substitution: in particular its conception of revelation yields some indication of the mystery of God, and some defense against facile and casual proofs or repudiations of God. Revelation theology may be able to survive for the time being on the basis of its concrete biblical statements and it may securely maintain its title to revelation by its radical and extensive rejection of the use of reason in matters of faith. By following this course, however, it necessarily arrives at a position in which its valuable insights are obscured, and even productive of negative consequences. Out of such revelation faith stems a dogmatism which is hostile to reason, a sophistical apologetic, i.e. an artful justification of hidden, undisclosed first premises.

The primary assertion of this theology is that the disjunction between God and world, revelation and reason—the absolute chasm between God's Word and man's word—can be spanned only at one point, namely in Jesus Christ.[13] Yet should we

[12] Paul Haeberlin defends this viewpoint. See, for instance, the brief formulation in his *Handbüchlein der Philosophie* (1949).

[13] The most rigorous representative of this "one-point theology" is now, as it has been, Karl Barth.

admit that this theology has correctly interpreted the intention of biblical revelation—it will be seen shortly that it is only partially correct—then it still would be necessary to question the authenticity of this biblical revelation and our capacity to comprehend it. Is this bridge of revelation earthly and historical or is it a supernatural, divine creation? Can one traverse it as a man or is it only a channel of the Holy Spirit? There are theologians who assert both at once: God's Word is not man's word; Christ is God; the Holy Spirit believes through us— and yet, at the same time, man's word expresses God's Word; Christ has come in the flesh; we ourselves must believe. Revelation is real; however, we cannot of ourselves comprehend this reality—thus, exactly the opposite of atheism and pantheism which assert that reality consists only in what we can grasp conceptually.

As we had to caution against absolutizing reason, so we must here fall back upon our reason to lead us again onto high ground, i.e. that capacity for knowledge by which I am conscious that *I*, and not another power, *my* intellect, and not the mind of God, perceives something—an intelligence certainly limited and capable of error, but also controllable and subject to correction. This latter corrective property of human ratiocination is eliminated and disavowed in revelation theology's dialectic of God's Word and human word, divine and human discourse. In consequence of this disavowal, divine and human utterance tend to flow into one another—and one can never say for certain where one ends and the other begins.[14] And therein lies the danger that God's Word will be degraded into human word, that human words will be given out as God's Word. Nor is such sacrilege only a dangerous possibility, for it occurs here and now. Despite their continual emphasis

[14] The document which most impressively illustrates this tendency is Karl Barth's "Prolegamena" to his dogmatics (*Church Dogmatics* I,1,2).

on the humanity of all our utterances, some theologians talk
as if they were lecturing to us from heaven on high—and
naturally there are always those who will dilute God's Word
because they think themselves freed in this convenient manner from all difficult questions and doubts.

We have become much too accustomed to "prophetic"
preaching and to pious platitudes. For when one perceives the
all too human personality that hides behind the prophet's
mantle, one becomes wary of this kind of utterance about God
—even at the risk of being attacked for unbelief. Nor can one
who knows anything at all about mass psychology have too
high an opinion of platitudes which are ostensibly filled with
the Spirit but in fact are merely the misguided products of
man's anxieties and longings.

However, our primary concern here is not the psychology
of faith, but rather the epistemological problem of reason and
revelation. With contemporary revelation theology, this problem is crystallized in the questions that emerge from its attempt to reach beyond its own internal presuppositions: i.e.
not only in the theoretical question of how such a faith can
arrive at an understanding of God in the face of its assertion
of the inadequacy of human reason, but also in the practical
question of how the Word of God can be preached to unbeliev-
ing man so that it will be acceptable to him. The response to
this problem by the type of revelation theology discussed thus
far has been one of almost compulsive avoidance—in fact, in
its refusal to face this problem it betrays the fear that it might
thereby undermine the platform from which it confidently
proclaims the Word of God. But far from securing its proclamation, this refusal has created many new anxieties and problems
for revelation theology.

Another version of revelation theology hopes to place itself
in the situation of the unbeliever and attempts to think and
question from his presuppositions. By revealing to him the un-

certainty of his knowledge and the hopelessness of his situation without God, it expects to make him tractable to the supernatural truths of revelation and, thus, to bring him to the point where he will not only recognize his otherwise unsatisfied desire for salvation, but also discover the consummation of his natural reason in revelation.[15] By using this method to remedy man's natural need for salvation, however, this theology, on the one hand, leaves itself perilously open to the Feuerbachian accusation that religion is an illusion and, on the other, in its attempt to see in the truths of revelation the fulfillment of rational modes of knowledge, offends against its own presupposition of the unprovability of God. For if this theology has accomplished some manner of proof of God, it is certainly not a proof immediately apparent to critical reason. Nor is this "proof," of course, decisive—the conclusions which theology of revelation has allegedly drawn from its mode of argumentation have been established from the beginning; these conclusions are in fact identical with its inherently inaccessible first principles. Therefore, it must be concluded that this theology, in order to secure salvation under the pressure of threatening difficulties, has merely surrendered the criteria with which it apparently agreed initially. This is a shaky pretext upon which to base something valued so dearly, and all the more so as this theology so prizes revelation. It must be said that a theology which depends on such an apologetic method surely cannot lead us to an authentic faith.[16]

We must acknowledge of this second version of the theology of revelation, as of that with which we dealt earlier, that despite its attack on reason, it can carry out its arguments only

[15] While in other ways they are very different, the theologies of Emil Brunner, Paul Althaus, Reinhold Niebuhr, Paul Tillich and even Rudolf Bultmann concur on this point.

[16] Thus Karl Barth passed judgment on Emil Brunner; see his *Church Dogmatics*, III,2, pp. 128 ff., and also III,4, pp. 19 ff.

with reason's help—unfortunately, with a reason essentially misunderstood and consequently abused.[17]

Having established this indispensable point of reference and having fixed these limits, let us now consider our own task of showing positively

3   How it is possible to speak rationally of God, but in a sense appropriate to the biblical conception of creation.

We are still faced with the limiting fact that God can be neither proved nor disproved, neither by reason nor by faith. Nor do reason and faith result from such an attempt, but rather irrationality and superstition. Irrationality and superstition, however, can be conquered by "believing reason" (*glaubige Vernunft*). Believing reason can avoid the false consequences of atheism and so-called revelation faith. It can bring itself to bear on legitimate concerns and can accede to a new and truly tenable understanding of the biblical conception of creation, to an accessible and truly acceptable faith in God, the creator. In order to develop the aspect of the reality of God that can be apprehended by reason and related to the biblical revelation of God as creator, we must ponder

[17] An argument that Martin Werner justly directed against this theology. See, for example, *"Das Prinzip der liberalen Theologie in der Gegenwart"* in *Schweiz Theologische Umschau* (1936), No. 4. See also Karl Jaspers, *Vernunft und Existenz*, translated as *Reason and Existence* (New York, Noonday Press, 1955), p. 109: "The denigration of thinking is still thinking, only a violent, reductive, constricted and self-blinding thinking."

A *How reason can and must speak of God.*

Reason, in essence, demands that all that men experience as rational creatures be brought together into an ordered whole. Reason achieves this unity by means of conceptual signs and logical deductions. We recognize a specific object because we can differentiate it from some other object: we fix distinctions so that we can order the various contents of our experience with appropriate concepts; then by means of such concepts, we hope to deal efficiently with similar experiences as they re-occur. All knowledge begins in naming, as is suggested in the biblical narrative of the creation in which it is said of Adam: "The man gave names to all cattle, and to the birds of the air, and to every beast of the field" (Gen. 2:20). All science depends on naming, the process of definition. With the assistance of a body of concepts we can understand and speak with one another, comprehend ourselves and one another.[18]

Yet the realm of concepts through which we communicate with each other is not the world as it exists independently of us—"in itself," as philosophy would say. It is rather a second world of our own creation, the created world of mental objects. This second world, moreover, is the sphere of truth, truth as it is expressed in unequivocal signs of experiential reality.[19]

[18] For a more detailed grounding in this theory of knowledge, we refer the reader to Moritz Sclick, *Allgemeine Erkentnislehre* (1925); also to Adolf Schlatter, *Das Christliche Dogma*, 2d ed. (1923), pp. 89 ff., and *Das Erkennen und die Wahrheit;* see also Friedrich Schneider, *Kennen und Erkennen* (1945), and *Erkenntnistheorie und Theologie* (1950).

[19] Karl Jaspers would see in this cognitive theory of conceptual truth, which, by the way, is not to be confused with the ethical conception of truth, only one kind of truth, namely, the cogent accuracy of "consciousness in general." But surely he would concede that other modes of knowledge can be discussed only in this objective, generally valid realm—even if one must always be conscious of its inadequacies in some of the circumstances in which it is applied. (See, for instance, his *Von der Wahrheit,* p. 231.) This limitation we thoroughly recognize, as will be pointed out in what follows; however, more emphatically than does Jaspers, we would affirm and seek to win recognition for the basic function of "truth for consciousness in general" in all our attempts to apprehend and to verify truth.

The main problem related to this understanding of how we experience reality consists in the clear and unambiguous application of our concepts. If such application is not warranted, "we spin airy chimeras, play games with reality, and draw further away from our goal"; therefore, our thoughts must always be reestablished in the experience from which their content derives. Reason, in the process of defining and drawing conclusions, must relate itself closely to reality. It must not become free-floating speculation.[20] Not only philosophy but also theology runs this risk, for theology also uses a special set of concepts in its utterances about God. If faith is not to be mere babble or happy chatter but "reasonable worship," as Paul asks of it (Rom. 12:1), then it must clearly and plainly say what it means.

Today God is not at home in either the philosophical or theological conceptual world. The Acts attributes the following words to Paul in Athens: "The God who made the world and everything in it, being Lord of heaven and earth, does not live in shrines made by men, nor is he served by human hands, as though he needed anything, since he himself gives to all men life and breath and everything" (17:24-5 ff.). Concepts produced by the human mind, even with the highest motives and most pious intentions, distort the reality of God: in fact, they promote worship of idols. In the realm of our thought and faith we do not reach God directly—we can only recognize God and speak of him with his assistance. The conceptions and imagery that we try to apply to God remain *our* conceptions, *our* images, *our* creations. What we fix in a thought is, and remains, *our* product—and in this process we construct a religion directly opposed to that intended by God. If we persist in speaking of God in such limited terms, we are only workers in an "idol factory."

[20] The dangers are illustrated, for instance, by the speculative "drawing-out" of the antecedents of the contents of experience in Aloys E. Biedermann's "pure realism." See the epistemological section of his *Christlichen Dogmatik*, 2d ed. (1884).

Whether pious or impious, we can speak of God only within the framework of our objective world and thus we do not deal directly with God but only with a derivative object of our reason; how can we break free from this vicious circle? We can liberate ourselves only by recognizing and accepting this situation, namely, that our notions of God are not God himself, that the human word is not God's Word. Yet at the same time we must continue to search, despite this inescapable difficulty, for a viable way to speak of God and of his revelation.[21] Two very distinct things must now be said.

First, we speak of God as we do because this is the way his Word has been communicated to us: we have all encountered God's Word in its traditional forms and have accepted it as it has been handed down to us. Doctrines and images of God are passed on to us and then passed on by us—whether or not they are understood or accepted, they must be preserved and conveyed to successive generations. They belong to our intellectual inventory, and we can only pity the man who is excluded, or who excludes himself, from the totality of this religious tradition.

Second, there are other sources for our statements about God, and while we must be cautious in our assumptions, we must still continue to question after the truth. The very diversity of past discussions of God compels us at all times to be wary of their uncertain status. We must be conscious always of the dubious nature of this whole enterprise. Its pitfalls are numerous; its problematic character leads some to stop speaking of God and to repudiate him; others use the occasion of speaking about God to hide timidly behind the external trappings of tradition.[22] We have demonstrated that atheism and

---

[21] Because it is arrested in neo-Kantian epistemology, for which the object of knowledge is merely a product of the process of knowing, dialectical theology stops short here and lapses into the circular dialectic of God's Word and man's word in order to evade the God-man.

[22] See Hans Schär, *"Erlösung durch das Gehäuse,"* in *Erlösungsvorstellungen und ihre psychologischen Aspekte* (1950), pp. 281 ff.

orthodoxy are untenable. We have nearly arrived at the point where we can begin to indicate, perhaps, some new sources for our present belief in God—so long as we ourselves resist the temptation to reach premature conclusions.

But what does it mean, in this connection, to resist? It means that we must take seriously the fact that reality is something other than our conceptual statements about it. Reality, to be sure, can only be distinguished from our ideas of it with difficulty. Once our words are applied to the real, they tend to exhaust its mystery, to imprison it within a concept and label it with a name—but in its essence the real remains something radically *other*. We can only know it to the extent that it declares itself to us, i.e. that it reveals itself to us clearly and distinctly. What is revealed to us, however, is not a full understanding of reality but only partial information about its nature: reality discloses itself to us ultimately as mystery. And this mystery at the heart of reality, even if we can point to it conceptually, is not of our own creation. Instead, we find ourselves standing before a reality which has been offered to our reason, which reason can understand and make significant only after the fact. Nor is this *after-the-fact* signification of our conceptal world *being-in-itself;* such signification is our own product and does not belong to the ultimate givenness of being. We have not produced *being-in-itself* but have only discovered ourselves in its context.[23]

There is no need for a long and complicated epistemological discussion to make us aware of the mystery of reality—although when such a discussion is carried on it inevitably terminates in such an awareness. Quite independently of all our talk about it, this mystery can startle us in the form of the question, Why, after all, is there something and not nothing? This question radically challenges all our familiar concepts and terms, which are dissipated in the face of an unfathomable

[23] See Martin Werner, *"Wesen und Wahrheit der Religion"* in *Das Ewige in der Religion* (Schwarzenburg, 1948), pp. 121 ff., *"Das Realitätsproblem."*

nothingness: it casts them into a fire in which they are destroyed or else from which they emerge purified and recast
into signs and images for expressing the unspeakable—symbols,
of course, which can be understood only in the context of the
primordial experience of religious persons. Belief in God originates in dangerous proximity to nihilism, and it always hovers
on the brink of this abyss when it is truly a living faith. Not
without good reason have the most profound religious thinkers
always spoken of the *Nothing*—not of an empty *Nothing*, but
rather of a *Nothing* filled with primary religious experience, the
creative *Nothing;* and thus we speak of God as the foundation and abyss of being—the creator God.[24]

The positive feature in the breakdown of all so-called proofs
of God which would pretend to make direct statements about
him lies in the fact that their failures reaffirm the ultimate
mysteriousness of his nature. And, thus, even the radical
atheism of our day promises a more accurate knowledge of
God in its silence than many who all too noisily proclaim
themselves capable of speaking about him. We must ask
revelation theology whether it interprets its speaking about
God in the sense outlined here or whether it chooses to rest
secure in pure mythology and, if this latter alternative, in
mere idolatry.[25]

On this basis, we must now expound

B   *The truth of the biblical conception of creation.*

When one speaks of the biblical conception of creation, there
come to mind immediately the first two chapters of Genesis
which are concerned with the creation of the world in six days,

[24] There is even a place in Jean Paul Sartre where he directs attention
to the mystery of being and depicts its fascination and terror. It is that
category-shattering experience of the *being* of a chestnut tree root in
Nausea.

[25] Martin Heidegger, not entirely incorrectly, states at the conclusion
of his book, *Was ist Metaphysik* (1931), that "letting-oneself-loose in the
Nothing" (*Sichloslassen in das Nichts*) means "liberation from the idols
which each of us has and secretly cherishes."

with the formation of the first man from a clod of earth. Until theology admitted that this conception is based in myth, a primitive attempt to explain the cosmos, it precipitated—with the rise of modern natural science and enlightened historical religious studies—many embittered battles between science and religion, between the modern conception of the world and biblical faith. These struggles over Darwin and Häckel, Bible and Babel, are now a part of the past—so much so that some theologians are again trying to bypass natural science's view of the first two chapters of the Bible and attempting to make them the basis of a modern theological doctrine of creation. Such theologians interpret the creation mythology as if it were somehow justified by the gracious covenant concluded in Christ.[26] This procedure is not only a slap in the face to those who see "natural science on the way to religion," but also betrays a mistaken understanding of the nature and significance of the biblical conception of creation.

Against this interpretation, for those of us who do not want to be lured into wild allegorizing, there are two essential and meaningful things to be said.

First, the creator does not stand over against his creation in absolute estrangement from it, an estrangement which is only bridged at one point in history, namely in Christ. While the creator enters his creation most fully at this point—in the incarnation of God—he still remains indissolubly connected with it as the creator of a universe which bears his manifest imprint, his indelible stamp. One cannot speak of the creator without the creation, nor of the creation without the creator. Both are inseparably connected with one another; one can discover God only in the world—a world, moreover, which cannot be understood without God.

[26] Such is the case with Karl Barth in his "Doctrine of Creation" (*Church Dogmatics*, III,1), whereas Brunner takes the problem of the relationship of religion and science much more seriously. See, for instance, his *Revelation and Reason* (Philadelphia, Westminster Press, 1946), p. 294, and *Dogmatik*, II, pp. 47 ff.

Second, in this indissoluble relationship there is to be discovered an inescapable, unconditionable, fundamental, distinction between the creator and his creation. The creator is and remains absolutely distinct from the creation. As creator he calls this world into being in a manner that defies any comprehensible analogy to the creative act as we are able to understand it. Nor does the creation, as it is actually accomplished by the creator, in any way represent some form of manifestation or emanation from God.

If the relationship of the creator with the created makes superfluous any attempt to bridge their apparent separation (a task sometimes asserted in the doctrine of the incarnation of God in Christ), the entrance of God into the world abolishes the supposedly necessary distinction between God and the world which is sometimes asserted as dogma. Theology which speculates about the ostensible explanation of the apparent miracle of the union of two natures, divine and human, in the incarnation of God in Christ would do better to apply its impressive formulas of *inseparability* and *unmixability* to the relation of God and his world. While in the former instance this theology offers elaborate explanations of an apparent problem, in the latter it casually assumes to be apparent what for us— in relation to the question of why something rather than nothing exists—remains the creative mystery of reality. God is not without his creation and the world is not without the creative depth of God—if, indeed, God and world are absolutely distinct from one another. The conception of creation is at once the most adequate formulation of our knowledge of God and of our understanding of his world.[27]

---

[27] In *Gottfried Kellers Glaube* (1944), pp. 93 ff., and *Gottfried Kellers Beitrag zu einer kunftigen protestantischen Wirklichkeitstheologie* (1944), pp. 16 ff., I have exhibited and commented on this immanence-transcendence relationship through examples from Keller's poetry—frequently poets know much more about the metaphysical depths of being than theologians. Martin Werner offers an excellent formulation of these issues in his *Thesen zum Christusproblem* (1934), pp. 13 ff., and *Wesen und Wahrheit der Religion*, pp. 133–41.

Obviously this, too, is still a mythological way of speaking—even if we neglect the six days' labor and Adam's rib. But perhaps it should not be held deficient on this count since we are not attempting a scientific explanation of the world. The myth of creation rather serves as a symbol for our existence in the world—a symbol which transcends all explanation, one which suddenly bursts forth in the midst of all explanation, and one which finally overwhelms our determined efforts to explain everything—for the secret of being, as such, simply cannot be explained.

On this basis, there is no conflict between natural science and the biblical conception of creation. As we know of no proof of God which overcomes his innate unprovability, so this proof of God represents no hypothesis of natural science. The truth of this concept of God cannot be contained on the plane of scientific knowledge; rather, it reaches vertically into another dimension. Discoverable in no worldly viewpoint, an authentic awareness of God supersedes any attempt to absolutize mundane perspectives.[28]

It is exactly by means of this awareness that the enduring problem of reason and revelation can be surmounted. This

[28] Kant not only views a proof of God as a postulate of practical reason and refers to God as a regulative idea of pure reason, but also sees such proofs as a potent expression of the confutation of reason in the face of the revealing mystery of being: "Unconditioned necessity, which we so indispensably require as the last bearer of all things, is for human reason the veritable abyss. Eternity itself, in all its terrible sublimity, as depicted by Albrecht von Haller [1708–77, poet and writer on medical and related subjects], is far from making the same overwhelming impression on the mind; for it only *measures* the duration of things, it does not *support* them. We cannot put aside, and yet also cannot endure, the thought that a being, which we represent to ourselves as supreme amongst all possible beings, should, as it were, say to itself: 'I am from eternity to eternity, and outside me there is nothing save what is through my will, but whence then am I?' All support here fails us. . . ." (*Critique of Pure Reason*, p. 513). Compare Karl Jaspers: "The conception of creation is the expression of a primordial mystery, the articulation of the incomprehensible, the subversion of the question by the uncaused cause" (*Reason and Existence*, p. 71).

problem only arises where reason is too highly regarded—namely, as the basis for a systematization of a self-enclosed world view—or where revelation is proposed as a power standing over against reason. But reason, according to the interpretation offered here, as it becomes aware in each instance of revelation and as it is the necessary basis of reality, must itself be viewed as a miracle—a miracle comparable to that of the creation. And for its part, reason must be clear about its status; it must not try to transcend its miraculous nature but rather do its thinking within the shadow of the miraculous. Reason must recognize both the limits and possibilities ordained by its own createdness, i.e. it must recognize itself as a never-ending, objectifying process of knowing which in each moment is nevertheless capable of advancing toward the creative mystery of reality.

This exposition cannot claim to have answered all the questions involved in man's attempt to speak of God, and with just cause both philosophical and theological critics may raise

4   Objections to this manner of speaking about God.

Philosophy—especially philosophy of religion and existential philosophy—may take exception to this decision to frame an answer to the question of God within the context of an analysis of the limits of man's capacity to know. It would maintain that the question of God is not theoretical at all, but rather that it originates at that point where man is aroused by the question

of right doing, where he seeks to discover the meaning of being
for his own existence, or, in religious terms, where he searches
for the will of God. For the religious believer, it would argue,
God is not simply the creative mystery of being but rather the
power which manifests its will to him as person, and which
reveals to him the meaning of his existence.[29]

And similarly, although on other grounds, biblical theology
would ask, What part is the revelation of God as creator to
play? Certainly it does not play as central a part as the redemptive revelation of God in Christ, for in that redemptive act God
manifests himself not as an impersonal mystery but rather as
the Father of Jesus Christ who gives his son to answer the
question, What ought I to do? [30]

Let us waste no time in acknowledging the justice of these
objections. They are mentioned simply to ward off any misun-
derstanding that might arise if it were assumed that the full
statement of our faith in God has now been presented. For an
awareness of the creative mystery of being is, of course, not
the only element in the Christian understanding of God. Without Christ in whom we discover the answer to the questions,
What ought I to do? and What may I hope? we certainly
could not speak adequately of God. Consequently, the preceding analysis represents only a preliminary development,
yet, as such, an essential prerequisite to what follows.

Only against the background of an understanding of God
as the mystery of the creative depth of being can the signifi-

[29] This is what Karl Jaspers means when he suggests that "universal"
transcendence must be regarded as "inauthentic," while "authentic"
transcendence refers only to existence (*Existenz*), i.e. in his sense can be
applied only in the questioning of human existence (*Dasein*), see *Von der
Wahrheit*, p. 109. See Fritz Buri, *Albert Schweitzer und Karl Jaspers*
(1950), pp. 22 ff.

[30] This is the position held today by Christo-centric theology under
the influence of Karl Barth, a theology which believes that the first
article of the Apostles' Creed should yield precedence to the second; and
for this reason Paul Althaus criticizes "Christo-monism" (*Die christliche
Wahrheit*, 1949, I, p. 68).

cance of revelation in Christ become apparent. For the alternative—an analysis stemming directly from the perspective of redemption—runs the risk of rendering innocuous the conception of the creator, and, what is worse, of arousing the suspicion that redemption itself is only an illusion, a postulated need. Christian faith only begins in belief in God; it is completed by belief in Christ and his kingdom. However, belief in the creator is prerequisite to belief in Christ, the subject of the next chapter.

Thus our analysis conforms with the order of the articles of belief of the Apostles' Creed. Summarizing what has been developed up to this point and looking ahead toward what is still to be considered, we confess in the words of the first article:

"I believe in God, the Father, Almighty, creator of heaven and earth."

Three

WHAT DOES CHRIST

MEAN FOR US?

The central question of the last chapter—How can we speak of God?—was brought to conclusion in the confession of the first article of the Apostles' Creed. Critical readers may consider such use of this credal formula unwarranted, or at least somewhat premature—and not without justification. For in speaking of God as Father, the Creed refers to far more than that thoroughly mysterious, creative ground at which we had arrived. The term *father*, applied to God, readily enables us to conceptualize him—a mode of conceptualization, however, that immediately conveys a wider set of attributes than our discussion can claim to have established. For *father* asserts not only God's mysterious nature but also thoroughly familiar paternal qualities; not simply boundless depth but also support and wisdom—and above all the love of the father who both accepts and protects his children.

These additional aspects of God are not, of course, implicit in the answer that was given to the theoretical question, How can we speak of God? They only become apparent from a practical or, perhaps more apt today, from an existential perspective, namely, in response to the question, What ought I to do so that my life will not be meaningless? It is in reference to this, the second of Kant's three questions introduced in the first chapter, that we can begin to speak authentically of God as Father.

For our sense of the fatherhood of God does not issue directly from his manifestation as creator but rather emerges from his revelation in Christ. As suggested in the previous chapter, while discussion of God as creator must anticipate the present account of Christ's revelation, we cannot speak adequately of God without Christ. Therefore, let us now turn to the question, What does Christ mean for us? in hopes that we shall be able to find an adequate answer to our central question, What ought I to do?

A direct appeal to the second article of the ancient Apostles' Creed will not yield us the answer we seek. As surely as the first article proclaiming God the Father, creator of heaven and earth, has nothing in itself to do with Christ, our contemporary confessional understanding of the Son cannot be expressed in the abstract terminology of the second article—God's only be-gotten son, our Lord, conceived of the Holy Ghost, born of the Virgin Mary, suffered under Pontius Pilate, crucified, dead and buried, descended into Hell, who on the third day arose again from the dead, ascended into Heaven, and sitteth at the right hand of God the Father, from whence he shall come to judge the quick and the dead.

We do not reject this credal description merely because it is incompatible with our own world view, but more signifi-cantly because it does not correspond to the appearance of Jesus Christ as it is rendered by the New Testament, and thus because it is fundamentally in error. This is not to say that it is wholly without value, for above all the Creed reminds us that Jesus Christ is not merely the extraordinary human being suggested by modern portrayals of the life of Jesus, and fal-lacious modernizations must be criticized just as rigorously as unscriptural orthodoxy for not accepting the results of current investigations into the native significance of Jesus Christ. Nor should the errors of present-day nihilism remain unchallenged —especially its surrender of the biblical proclamation to his-torical relativism; concomitantly, orthodoxy's failure to ac-knowledge and thus avoid these errors of nihilism must be shown to be contrary to its own announced goals.

These preliminary postulates and guidelines are an indispensable stage in this analysis, for only on such a basis can the significance of the biblical Christ be stated and the meaning of his proclamation for our own time be appraised. Nor does the focus of this chapter fully exhaust the issues raised by the question, What ought I to do? An additional perspective as vital to orthodoxy and nihilism as to us must be left for later consideration, namely, that suggested by the question, What may I hope? And thus the final stage in our presentation is reserved for the following chapter.

Guided by this outline of the challenges with which we are faced, we can now begin to examine

1   What can no longer be disregarded in any authentic understanding of the meaning of the Christ.

Perhaps we can best bring our central question into focus by evaluating the results produced by scientific investigation of the New Testament's proclamation and its subsequent fate in history. Research findings, obviously, are never complete or definitive. Any absolute claim for their results would immediately divest them of their scientific character, for science cannot guarantee its positive conclusions; its findings are always being extended. But through research some progress is unquestionably made in expanding human knowledge. In time facts fall into place which must be dealt with and which may prove costly to ignore; on the basis of such facts we must continue to question our fundamental assumptions.

Since it is no longer possible to disregard the methods of historical research nor to revoke its conclusions, two significant judgments regarding the proclamation of the Christ in the New Testament must be noted. First, the figure of Christ belongs fully to history with all its contingencies; no phenomenon apparent to man can escape the historical dimension. Second, despite the threat of historical relativism and although Christ's significance cannot in the least be grasped by science, the power embodied in the figure of Christ is manifest throughout history.[1] It is the first of these two judgments that nihilism has seized upon, wielding the completely uncertain character of human history against the admittedly problematic question of an historical Jesus and an historical Gospel. And orthodoxy, for its part, has argued from the second judgment in that it depends upon its doctrine of redemption in Christ to safeguard the so-called supra-historical Jesus.

We must next expose

A *The radical disintegration of the dogma of Christ in history as well as its alleged nihilistic consequences.*

The classical God-man dogma of the Christ has always stressed both aspects of the saviour's nature—his divinity as well as his humanity. Theology has usually measured Christ's natural humanity against his supernatural divinity, and it has viewed the incarnation of God in human form as only one moment in the divine process of redemption. Theologians have, however, tended to oscillate between a divinization of Jesus' humanity, which leads to a doctrine of two gods, and a reduction of his human nature to mere illusion, which negates the reality of his redemptive sorrow and death. For the classical dogmatists, in any event, Christ did not represent a human personality to be grasped through historical science, but rather an elusive supernatural power. Christ was viewed as a sacro-

[1] See my article, *"Christus gestern und heute"* in *Schweiz. Theol. Umschau* (1948), pp. 97 ff.

sanct divine norm somehow manifest in the midst of history, an instrument through which the believer might attain that eternal realm located beyond all worldly uncertainty.

Since the Enlightenment, men have dared to reexamine the figure of the Christ previously relegated to heavenly splendor, and by applying human categories have restored it to the realm of natural history.[2] Unfortunately, this process of reinterpretation has subjected the significance of the Christ to radical distortions and has tended to reduce it to the commonplace. The first historical critics had to learn to reformulate specific doctrines with precision—and here they could profit greatly from the false starts and mistakes of the past—and continally they had to remind themselves that an examination of the figure of Christ presents extraordinarily challenging problems. In the course of the nineteenth and early twentieth centuries, this attempt to approach the New Testament through historical investigation yielded wholly new research methods and conclusions that have subsequently become standard features of historical science. With these new tools of research Jesus and his Gospel were reinterpreted in the context of their own times and social environment, and their effects came to be understood in relation to the universal history of mankind.

· One consequence of the prevailing supernaturalism of dogma and its related faith in redemption had been the assumption that Jesus could and should be viewed as a unique, if unearthly and eternal, incarnation. His ideal humanity, it was assumed, eclipsed all other powers in history. The deduction of divine norms from a reading of history was another characteristic tendency of earlier times. But as the principles of historical research were consistently applied and the hypothetical character of all its results was gradually acknowledged—when it was realized that historical judgments are always made from some particular standpoint and that there

2 Such is the plain intent of Albert Schweitzer's *The Quest of the Historical Jesus.*

can be no special exemptions from the continuing process in which all objects of history are mutually conditioned—the defense of the old order of understanding became all but untenable. Historical powers were virtually leveled in significance, certainly made precarious, and seriously threatened by relativism.

The problems raised by historical science became most acute for the comprehension of the figure of Jesus and of Christianity in general at the point where the original phenomena were extracted from their narrower sources in the Bible and in Western history and reconsidered within the broader matrix of the ancient Near Eastern religious climate as well as that of other world religions. All at once, dependencies and correlations in motive and conception, in developmental law and the formation of dogma, became apparent and seemingly obviated any further claims for the originality of Jesus or for the absolute character of Christianity.

But it was the emergence of the eschatological viewpoint as the consequence of religious historical research that fundamentally unsettled the once secure standing of Christian theology. The most disturbing challenge, perhaps, came in the form of Albert Schweitzer's "thoroughgoing" eschatological interpretation of Jesus and of primitive Christianity, indeed, of the whole history of Christendom.[3] According to Schweitzer, Jesus can be explained entirely in terms of the expectation of redemption common to his contemporary Near Eastern community, an expectation stemming out of the late Judaic apocalyptic vision. What Jesus borrowed from this general expectation of the last days and actualized in himself was its messianic consciousness of the ethical personality. All his moral admonitions, even his seemingly distinctive acts, must be seen

[3] See Albert Schweitzer, *The Mysticism of Paul the Apostle,* trans. by William Montgomery (New York, Henry Holt and Co., 1931), and also Martin Werner, *The Formation of Christian Dogma* (London, A. & C. Black, 1957).

merely as a reflection of this widespread expectation of the imminent end of this world. What was truly unique for Jesus and his community in this eschatologically minded climate, namely the passion with which he conceived the idea of the end and in which he lived towards its coming, proved to be foolishness in the eyes of the world because history, itself, repudiated the fulfillment of the eschatological promises; the history of this hope was in time converted to a history of prolonged despair.

As radical as was this denouement for the eschatological hope, the dogma of the God-man saviour could not be undermined; but at least for the time being, it is this new notion of the deluded saviour that represents the last in the long series of historical-scientific interpretations of Jesus, the outcome of the whole evolution of historical research.[4]

Thus it is no small wonder that today nihilism declares: nothing is absolute; everything is relative; it makes no difference what one does; life has no meaning. Nihilism feels that nothing can be done about the fact that its attitude reduces all greatness to the commonplace. If it takes any notice at all of Christianity, if it has not long ago relinquished all interest in Christ's special significance as a result of the general relativizing of history, it believes its reductive viewpoint vindicated by the consequences of historical research. Isn't nihilism at least in part an offshoot of Schweitzer's "thoroughgoing" eschatological interpretation of Jesus?

We shall have to prove that the above conclusions of nihilism are fallacious; but we should be grateful to this movement, for it provides a potent antidote to false romanticism about Jesus— whether it be dogmatic or undogmatic. A tinge of scepticism is not to be despised, for it offers immunity to that total nihilism which diminishes its own best insights by the refusal to recognize its own truly authentic moments. For

[4] See Fritz Buri, *"Das Problem der ausgebliebenen Parusie,"* in *Schweiz. Theolog. Umschau* (1946), pp. 97 ff.

B   *Orthodox theology with its emphasis on Christ as other
than a real man*

does not manifest just a tinge of scepticism, but rather a totally
nihilistic evaluation of natural man. This attitude on the part of
orthodoxy, grounded as it is in the Reformation interpretation
of the dogma of original sin, cannot be attributed to modern
nihilism. Certainly the reformers were not in complete agreement about the import of this doctrine, nor were they as individuals completely unequivocal in tracing its implications. On
the one hand the reformers proclaimed the absence of human
merit and the total corruption of human nature in the fall of
Adam in order to stress the sole efficaciousness of grace in the
process of redemption. On the other hand they recognized the
problems raised for the doctrine of redemption by a complete
repudiation of human worth; redemption would become a
purely external, magical event if it could not be linked with
justification, with man's desire for redemption, and thus with
some measure of cooperation in the process of salvation on
the part of man's natural powers.[5]

Occasionally, then, the reformers admitted that man might
retain—even after the fall—a residue of the divine likeness to
which the commands of God and the grace of the Gospel
could appeal. It was agreed—since the Bible would seem to
indicate it!—that even a sinner is something more valuable
than a stone or a cat; but in contrast to the Roman Catholic
Church, which had maintained that man is at least in part
uncorrupted by the fall and that a lingering element of man's
original goodness can cooperate with God's redeeming grace,

[5] Emil Brunner, not only on epistemological grounds but also for the
sake of ethical consequences, is especially concerned at the starting point
about the extent to which the divine likeness has survived in natural
man, and also directs his attention to the "orders of creation." See *"Das
Gebot und die Ordungen"* in his *Ethik* (Tübingen, J.C.B. Mohr, 1932),
or his anthropology in *Der Mensch im Widerspruch,* trans. by Olive
Wyon as *Man in Revolt* (New York, Charles Scribner's Sons, 1939).

the reformers tended to emphasize the total bankruptcy of the human condition.

It is on the basis of this Reformation heritage—man is nothing, grace everything—that current orthodoxy from a nihilistic standpoint condemns idealism and humanism alike, that it adopts nihilism as its ally against liberal theology. Assuming these nihilistic attitudes widespread in contemporary drama and literature to reproach liberal theology for its lack of modernity and realism, orthodoxy charges that liberal theology clings to untenable illusions about humanity, that it overlooks man's desperate lack of solid foundations, man's state of total deprivation.[6] Even to orthodoxy's devout adherents this attack on liberal theology must seem a bit cynical.

In posing its own solution to the hopeless situation of man, orthodoxy accepts the thesis of "thoroughgoing" eschatology —that Jesus and the New Testament writers were deceived in their expectation of the coming of God's kingdom. In fact, orthodoxy not only uses the eschatological viewpoint to assert that a purely scientific reconstruction of the history of Jesus and his proclamation—even one not based in faith—must reach this conclusion, but it also finds Jesus in error and, measured against history, a total failure. Despair and failure, then, are to be the inescapable destiny of man in his struggle for life.

Thus, current orthodoxy sustains the pessimism inherent in the doctrine of original sin, the *malaise* in the spirit of our time, and the submission of the New Testament's eschatological hope to critical analysis because it rests its case wholly upon the supernatural redemptive event which occurred in and through the Christ, and which it believes still shapes the cosmos. The Christ, according to its view, does not even fundamentally belong to the human sphere: his humanity was only adopted. If his redeeming work took place in history, it

[6] See Karl Barth's reference to Jean Paul Sartre in *Church Dogmatics*, III, 3, pp. 338 ff.

does not continue to unfold in the historical dimension but rather conquers history.

If its peculiar interpretation of the doctrine of the person and work of Christ is dubious—we shall attempt to show why in detail later—there is no question that orthodoxy holds a thoroughly correct view of the New Testament when it sees in the Christ a divine being, and in his saving work, a supernatural history. For the religious-historical and eschatological perspectives have opened our eyes precisely to the mythological character of the Gospel. Surely Jesus of Nazareth who, according to the first three evangelists, expected to reappear imminently as the Messiah coming on the clouds of heaven, or in whom, according to Paul, a heavenly being had been humbled, was a mere man. But the Christ, the son of David, the son of God, the Lord (*Kyrios*)—the titles given to the saviour in the New Testament—signified a divine being originating out of the eternal, as did the title, son of Man, a symbol for the understanding of the Messiah as an angelic being.[7] The redemption which God accomplished through this being whom he had established as his instrument was indeed a cosmic event, a drama spanning heaven and earth.

Consequently, the Christ may seem strangely mythological in comparison with the more familiar figure of the human Jesus; and while it may seem more natural to honor Jesus simply as the greatest teacher—perhaps even as the greatest man—the second article of the Apostles' Creed and its present-day confessors actually stand closer to the Christianity of the New Testament than did the old liberal devotees of Jesus. The eschatological Christ is a mythological, divine being, and in this understanding both contemporary research and orthodox Christology are in fundamental accord.[8] The mythological

[7] See Martin Werner, *The Formation of Christian Dogma*, pp. 120 ff.

[8] A typical representative of both the mythological interpretation and of orthodoxy is Rudolf Bultmann. See *Kerygma and Myth*, Hans Werner Bartsch, ed. (London, S.P.C.K., 1954).

character of the Christ, no less than the historical uncertainty of eschatology which offers potential inroads to nihilism, has been confirmed in our time by a body of settled knowledge which can no longer be repudiated.

This judgment, however, must be immediately followed by a careful appraisal of

2 The fallacies of both nihilism and the orthodox doctrine of redemption.

A *The intrinsic inconsistencies of nihilism*

can be broadly established without any special reference to the unfulfilled promise of the imminent end of history enunciated in the New Testament. For nihilism asserts that there is neither truth nor meaning to be discovered in human existence; we neither can nor ought to take a stand in life—no human decision is of any consequence. Nihilism takes this stance against all its critics. And since in our statements about matters which mean a great deal to us we are easily tempted into overstatement by strong feelings or anxieties—overstatement which is especially liable to critical examination— nihilism easily exposes the all-too-human limits of our metaphysical, theological and ethical systems. It punctures the relative, the conditioned, the dubious elements in our absolutes; and thus it frees itself from the obligation of finding original grounds for its own theses.

But useful and necessary as such a corrosive critique may be for insuring the distinction between the real and the un-

real, the true and the false, nihilism betrays its own fundamental error in at least one basic respect, i.e. whenever it
claims that its critique is adequate. Patently, the nihilistic
critique must also make a claim to truth. Further, the nihilist's
claim that no human decisions are of any consequence is itself a human decision and quite obviously, a matter of some
consequence to the nihilist, if, indeed, this is what he chooses
to urge upon us. Thus, at the point where the nihilist has de-
cided in favor of nihilism he has already left nihilism behind—
at least a nihilism understood as obviating the necessity for
making decisions. In short, no one can *be* a nihilist, for nihilism as a way of life is a self-contradiction.

This conclusion has basic and general validity. If nihilism
now redirects our attention to the questionable status of all
human powers in history as a justification for its own position
(for instance, if it points to the idiosyncratic character of the
various manifestations of Christianity, or particularly to the
problem of Christianity's origin in the disappointed expectation of the kingdom of God held by Jesus and his community), we must point out in return that the Christian
expectation of the kingdom is not a proof for, but rather
evidence against, the claims of nihilism.

While it is certainly true that history's departure from the
course predicted by Jesus and the early Christian Church is
an indication of the uncertainty of all human designs and un-
dertakings (and thus prone to nihilistic interpretation) nevertheless the conception of the kingdom of God, itself, the
expectation of its coming, the personal pledge for its realization, are antithetical to nihilism; they represent a decision and
a pledge in behalf of a goal which has emerged directly out of
an awareness of the complete uncertainty of finite history, a
goal which is in fact the conquest of history. This conquest,
at least in the form in which it has been anticipated, may fail
entirely. But the fact that in this instance history is questioned

for the sake of its meaning, that a position is taken and maintained in the face of unleashed demonic powers, suffering, and death so that a new order of perfection may be realized not only for selfish purposes, but for others as well—such a radical commitment makes nihilism's indifference and sterility seem pitiful by comparison. To what other end but the betrayal of man's most promising potentialities does nihilism claim the right to cast aspersions on all established values, to substitute its purely negative insights for accepted meanings, especially since this substitution is predestined to failure by the innate self-contradictions of nihilism itself? The possibilities for history manifested in the eschatological vision, and particularly its realization in Jesus and the primitive Christian community, confront nihilism with a decision as to whether or not it can afford to depend on its own negative insights and critical powers. And because nihilism must make some positive decisions, it will be ultimately overwhelmed. It must be hot or cold, for if it remains only lukewarm, it will be spat out in disgust, as John suggests in his letter to the seven churches (Rev. 3:16).

But no less self-contradictory than nihilism,

B The untenable orthodox doctrine of redemption

stands opposed to the real eschatological Christ. Orthodoxy clearly pursues the line of reasoning of "thoroughgoing" eschatology: Christ is viewed as more than the mere man proclaimed by earlier liberal theology. He is granted the supra-worldly, divine status to which Jesus was elevated after his death—or whose appearance he already represented during his lifetime. But if it is to be assumed that eschatology offers a new prop for the God-man dogma of classical Christian theology, two crucial relations must be distinguished: the relation of Jesus of Nazareth to the person of the Christ and the relation of both to God. For each of these relations is

differently conceived in the New Testament than in the subsequent dogmatic accounts of Christ's divine and human natures and of the God-man's relation to God the Father.[9]

The Trinitarian-Christological debates regarding the relation of the divinity of God to the divinity of Christ and the
dogma of the two natures in Christ which the ancient church
vehemently argued for hundreds of years, are concerns entirely foreign to the New Testament. In fact, the New Testament offers no hint of challenge to monotheism by some
supposed competition between the divinity of God and the
divinity of the Christ—for in the New Testament Christ is
conceived as only one of the heavenly angelic beings—one
who is predestined and summoned by God as Messiah and
entrusted with the task of the new creation. Either the relationship of Jesus to this angelic being is represented in terms
of his reappearance as this being at the end of time or the
Christ is understood as that being which sometime earlier had
adopted Jesus' form. How either alternative might be possible
was not a matter of concern, for the biblical mentality easily
assumed, and especially in its eschatological speculations, that
angels can take on human form and that men can be elevated
into heavenly beings.

This understanding of the Christ first raised problems for
the ancient Church when doubts were cast upon the redemptive significance of the death of Christ by the prolonged delay
in the anticipated end. Originally it had been thought that his
death would signal the final disintegration of this world and
the advent of God's kingdom. This expectation, which had
guided Jesus to Jerusalem, and which he had even proclaimed
there publicly, was further sounded in the events which Matthew supposed should have taken place immediately after his
death, or in the events that Matthew did record: the curtain

[9] For what follows, reference may again be made to Martin Werner's
The Formation of Christian Dogma.

of the Temple tore, the earth shook, graves opened and the bodies of the saints rose from the dead and appeared in the city. In this context, the testimony concerning Jesus' own resurrection belongs to the beginning of the last days.

But even the events which were reported only faintly echoed what had been anticipated as the effects of Jesus' death. The end did not actually occur; history continued. Even in the oldest sources, attempts were made to explain the uncertainties raised by the death; but whatever significance we now attribute to the cross must be radically different from that originally ascribed to it, for the eschatological prediction has not really been fulfilled.

It is not our primary concern to pursue the various reconstructions of the New Testament's doctrine of Christ's works and person as they are projected through the whole history of dogma. As an important stage in this process of reinterpretation, we would only note the origin of the institutionalized version of redemption initiated by the Catholic Church. Catholicism assimilated the historical fact that the kingdom of God did not immediately dawn with the death of Jesus; it perceived that this event marked rather the beginnings of the Church. Even if Jesus had not explained history accurately, still the Church, and consequently his saving work, could endure. The work of salvation, according to the views of the Church fathers, no longer consisted in the establishment of a new eon, but rather in the guarantee of the saintly life and of immortality on the basis of the sacraments. The decisive change was no longer anticipated as an imminent cosmic event—the end of the world when Christ would return was projected into the distant future. In the meantime, the role of the Church would be to dispense the sacraments entrusted to it. By the transubstantiation of the bread and wine in the Mass the redeeming event would be fulfilled, and in this celebration the believer might become a participant in the redemption of Christ. The ancient Church fathers were claiming in effect that man could deify his mortal nature by partaking of the sacraments.

If the sacraments were to have such extraordinary powers, the Christ could not be depicted simply as an angelic being subordinate to God; he must become God himself. On the basis of the miraculous redemptive works attributed to him, Christ was thus elevated to divinity, a status which has subsequently troubled theology as it has endeavored to determine Christ's exact relation to the divinity of God. This symbolic mode of interpreting Christ as God emerged suddenly in the New Testament in the Gospel which also discloses the first traces of the God-man doctrine of redemption—the Gospel of John which concludes with Thomas addressing the resurrected Jesus as "my Lord and my God."

This doctrine of the divine-humanity of Christ was eventually elevated to dogma and accepted uncritically, even by the reformers. To be sure the reformers vehemently denounced and repudiated the magical sacramental view of redemption because it supported the Catholic doctrines of sainthood and merit. But if the Reformation replaced the latter doctrines with "justification by faith alone," it did not, as it intended by this modification, thereby simply return to the biblical, and especially the Pauline conception of redemption. On excellent grounds the Catholic Church has continued to point out that the central Protestant doctrine of justification is not only questionable from an ethical perspective but unscriptural as well.

It is true that in his disputes with the Jews, Paul challenged the validity of Jewish cultic laws and the possibility of perfecting self in the eyes of God merely by good works. He reached this conclusion because, as he put it, the Judaic law belongs to the old world overcome by Christ. Paul even believed that Jewish righteousness could be challenged as a device of the demons, who used its institutional obligations to bind men under their dominion, and who sought thereby to undermine the victory of Christ. Never did it occur to Paul, however, to base his ethics on this doctrinal debate, nor could he have shared Luther's confidence that "no matter how great the sin, God's grace is still greater." According to Paul, Christ atoned in his death only for the sins of those who had lived before the institution of baptism (Rom. 3:25). With the advent of baptism, therefore, the believer's saintliness must be tested, because in baptism he has supposedly died with Christ to this world and henceforth the powers of the resurrected world should flourish in him and prepare him for doing good works on the basis of which he can endure judgment at Christ's second coming.

It is in this context that the Catholic doctrines of grace and merit still offer valuable insights even if the Catholic Church has substituted its own dominion for that of the heavenly kingdom. The Reformation doctrine of justification, however, falls into its greatest difficulties at this point. In response to the question, What ought I to do? it can only say to men: "Our acts are to no purpose, even in the best life," or, that to live with grace means, as Luther once said, "Sin boldly but believe still more strongly, and enjoy yourself!" We should still like to discover the profound truth hidden in this scandalous statement. If, as is the case with orthodoxy today, Luther was attempting to base the dogmas of the divinity of Christ, his incarnation, and vicarious justification on the shaky foundations of the primitive Christian eschatological hope of redemption, then surely he contributed to the relativizing of all ethics, in fact, to the support of nihilism.

Thus we must reject the orthodox doctrine of redemption insofar as its unscriptural distortions and its anti-ethical tendencies link it to nihilism. For nihilism and orthodoxy alike fail to acknowledge

3   The actual fact of redemption intended by the primitive conception of the Christ.

Having rejected these erroneous formulations, we must examine the reality of Christ as the special revelation of God, the reality in which the creative mystery of being of which we spoke in the last chapter first manifests itself as that to which we may legitimately apply the designation Father.

Let us begin by elucidating

A   *The reality of Christ in the New Testament*

so that we proceed to inquire what this reality can mean for us. According to what has been said thus far, a sharp distinction must be drawn between the Christ and Jesus. Jesus surely understood himself as the Christ elected to come, and his immediate community worshipped him as this Christ. But even though the two names were united in Jesus as the Christ, they did not simply indicate the same phenomenon. Jesus of Nazareth was a human personality, while the Christ represented a supernatural divine being. For the classical prophets, the Messiah (Christ is the Greek translation of the Hebrew word for the anointed messiah) was to come as a mythical king, born of David's stock to rule over the last days. Later, as Judaism played out its political destiny, the Messiah was anticipated as a heavenly, angelic being (the son of Man of the books of Daniel and Enoch). He was also described as a suffering, dying and resurrected saviour. These diverse conceptions of the Messiah seem to have been unified by Jesus, in that he viewed himself concurrently as the descendant of David's line, as the one destined to come from God, and as the son of Man elected to return upon the clouds of heaven. Further, he believed that he could ransom himself for this future glory through suffering and death; at any rate his community subsequently understood him in terms of this mythological-eschatological world view.[10]

We must not be misled into identifying too readily the mythological powers of the Christ with the historical person of Jesus. Even the New Testament record does not restrict the locus of the Christ merely to Jesus but suggests a much wider dominion. For Paul as for John, the Christ is hidden in the eternal: surely, they proclaim, he existed at the creation of the world (John 1:1; Col. 1:16; Heb. 1:2; and Prov. 8:22). According to Paul he accompanied the people of Israel on its journey through the wilderness and was manifest in the water-giving rock (I Cor. 10:4). For Paul, the resurrected body is not the body of the earthly Jesus but rather a spiritual body, and this body of Christ expands to include the society of all elected believers, all those who will be resurrected as the mystical body of Christ, and this latter conception was eventually identified with the existing church as the body of Christ, the communion of saints (e.g. Rom. 6:8).

Thus the concept of the Christ in the Bible is a symbol of a special creative intervention of God through which the first, incomplete creation and its powers are overturned and replaced by a new, perfected creation under God's sovereign authority. The Christ is the active cause of this new creation and thus the instrument by which God accomplishes the eschatological end of an era in the course of a uniquely prepared, supernatural, redemptive history. The Christ is also the principle of life which governs the new creation, is himself the salvation of this wholly new dominion. As Paul says of the

[10] Rudolf Bultmann also distinguishes between the exhortation of the historical Jesus and the proclamation of the Christ to the early Christian community. See the introduction to his *Theology of the New Testament* (New York, Charles Scribner's Sons, 1951–55).

beginning of the end of time: "For from him and through him and to him are all things" (Rom. 11:36).

This messianic mythology permeates the whole Bible. It is not just a biblical concept, but is encountered elsewhere in various forms in the history of religions. Since Jesus applied it concretely to his own life and destiny, the New Testament writers sought to comprehend and communicate the significance of Jesus in the context of this mythology, and in this process of interpretation, the myth of the Christ acquired a thoroughly distinctive character, first of all through Jesus himself, but also through the contributions of his contemporary community, and especially of Paul and John.

If, for example, the presently accepted accounts of the words of Jesus and actions corresponding to them in the canon of the first three Gospels are compared, along with other contemporary apocalyptic notions and religious practices, to later accretions in the Church, vast changes from the original milieu can be discovered. This, then, is perhaps the place where it becomes both possible and necessary to discuss the person of Jesus. In his understanding and reinterpretation of the traditional accounts of the end, in his view of his own role as Messiah, and in his endurance of death, Jesus proved himself to be a powerful ethical, religious and prophetic personality. In the Sermon on the Mount he exposed the Jewish righteousness which had granted itself hypocritical license to escape the gravity of its disobedience of God's commands; he reaffirmed man's inevitable confrontation with the Holy God. He reformulated the divine principle that to preserve life is good and to destroy it, evil (Mark 3:4). He not only reminded men of their shame before God but also assured God's pardon to the sinner who acknowledged his own guilt and proclaimed the restoration to life offered by God which would enable men to redirect their actions in accordance with a new sense of righteousness—the gift from which the power to forgive our own transgressions accrues.

Through the powers granted to him, Jesus took upon himself the same bodily necessities as his fellowmen and in compassionate sympathy also assumed their burdens, the guilt and need of the world, which had been irreconcilable with God's omnipotence and love and from which had sprung both his conviction of the imminence of final redemption and his readiness to sacrifice his own life.

That his ultimate hope was rooted in personal experience is apparent from the fact that scriptural analysis was not merely a speculative interest for him—scripture rather suggested a present declaration for his own time. The proximity of redemption called for immediate personal response—in fact demanded it unconditionally. Thus Jesus went to his death in behalf of those who might be spared—to overcome the last resistance of the demons, to abate the evils of this world in himself. By his suffering and the sacrifice of his own person he hoped to absolve the guilt which had checked the coming of God's kingdom. Interpretation of his suffering as sacrifice freed him from anxiety so that he might go to his death with an inner sense of liberation from the cares of this world.[11]

As his disciples ever afterwards would be persuaded by his resurrection, there was reflected in Jesus' faith the conviction that his life had been so lived that its meaning could not be destroyed by its extrinsic failure. To the contrary, it was to be fulfilled precisely in its denouement. Most of us who find ourselves drawn to the greatness of the person of Jesus and who live and ourselves suffer in the context of our relationship to his spirit, endeavor to repent and practice love; we share with Paul the sense that "If we live we live to the Lord, and if we die we die to the Lord; so then, whether we live or whether we die, we are the Lord's" (Rom. 14:8). For the

---

[11] See the account given by Albert Schweitzer in *Geschichte der Leben-Jesu-Forschung* (Tübingen, J.C.D. Mohr, 1913). The relevant portion cited here is omitted from the English translation, *The Quest of the Historical Jesus.*

men of Jesus' day these words were not as they have become for us—a burial formula—but rather a truth of life. The atonement of the cross with its suffering and shame liberated men from the anxieties of their own lives and guided them to the reality of a new life of forgiveness and freedom to forgive others. As John proclaimed, "We know that we have passed out of death into life, because we love the brethren" (I John 3:14).

Christians have used the mythological elements of this eschatology to express and declare the New Being, and, reshaping it into creeds and dogmas, have further extended the mythological mode of expression. But wherever Christianity is a truly living faith and not—as for the apostles prior to Pentecost—a mere external framework upon which man anxiously depends for support, these mythological symbols must become a unique expression of personal witness and experience. Apart from its manifestation in our own lives, the reality of the Christ can have no meaning for us.

There is, however, more that must be said about

B   *The reality of Christ for us.*

This reality, as we have analyzed it, does not disclose itself to us so as to enable us to relive the New Testament witness or any of its subsequent reformulations: we cannot demonstrate or prove the truth of this reality. As the epistemological discussion of the first chapter established, images and words do not in themselves guarantee the reality which they signify; such an assumption would only encourage the primitive "word magic" all too frequently practiced in present-day church preaching. Rather, images and words flow out of reality, a reality which we do not ourselves produce but which proclaims itself to us in our personal experience. We can relate Christian signs and symbols to the contents of our experience through reflection and meditation, and thus sustain and clarify their significance and communicate it to others. But no more than our forms of expression can in themselves yield up reality to us, can we use our Christian conceptions to convince others of the reality of Christ. The special reality of our concepts consists in their indication of the part we play in shaping our own experience; and for others as well, the value of our symbolic expressions lies in their reminder of the continual process through which experience originates out of ourselves.

It is such an epistemological understanding that must be applied consistently to the Christian symbolism and the world of thought stemming out of it. The Gospel issued from the primitive community's shared experience; its proclamation must be viewed by us as a potential factor in our own experience. As we usually come to understand each other when our words derive their significance from a common basis in experienced reality, so it is also incumbent upon us to share Christ's mental world in order to grasp the meaning of his words. We first begin to understand him correctly when his words disclose to us some aspect of our own experienced reality. Thus, the myth of Christ, in the form in which Jesus, and subsequently his followers, communicated it, can become a symbol of salvation in our own world; but the key to our understanding of the Christ lies ultimately in ourselves.

Christ's reality emerges for us where we live and act, as we perceive it in practice around us, when we no longer simply say "Yes" but become conscious of its uncertainty as well as its perfection, its peril and shame, its risk and ruin. This is not to say that we can no longer perceive other springs of goodness, of beauty, of greatness in our lives in the world apart from Christ—values for which we may be grateful. On the contrary, we suffer the pangs of meaninglessness and failure precisely because we are aware of such significance and calling in our lives. It is the very significance that we discover in being that makes it problematic. And the crisis of meaning-lessness becomes acute exactly where we recognize this signifi-cance—the crisis from which the eschatological viewpoint can emerge and again become relevant to human affairs. Nor can we allow the eschatological apprehension to obscure the grav-ity of the crisis of history; to use it as the tool of some deriva-tive theory of redemptive history would only be to encourage a false solution to the crisis. The crisis must be acknowledged and borne in its utter seriousness, as Jesus avowed: "Who would follow me, must take up his cross . . ." (Mark 8:34). Our participation in the peace that "higher is than all reason" (Phil. 4:7) can neither be commanded by force nor guaran-teed; it can only be experienced as a free gift—a gift not always granted. Only when we have abandoned our senseless protest against what must be endured—or against recognition of our own guilt—and have instead rendered homage to God, will our anxiety and guilt be softened.[12]

And precisely because suffering as well as the capacity to bear life's burdens, to make new beginnings, to exist, in fact, are grace as we experience it, nihilistic defiance and orthodox redemptive magic must be rejected. Where grace abounds we are made free, and become capable of that love, depicted by Paul in the thirteenth chapter of I Corinthians, which does not demand its own way. In this understanding we experience death and resurrection with Christ and the New Being of which the epistles of his most notable apostle, Paul, give such vital evidence. It is at this point that Paul's doctrine of justi-fication in the form that Luther gave it of "righteous and sin-ner together" can express the power of God's unmerited, liberating grace.

Certainly this viewpoint is not limited to Jesus Christ and the realm of symbols and sensibility connected to his name.

[12] Compare the experience of grace in the theology of the cross of the young Luther as I have described it in *Kreuz und Ring* (1947).

"The spirit blows where it listeth." The reality of Christ is not
restricted to its formal expression in the Bible or in the Church,
and it is always a sign of failure in either a church or a theology when it supposes that salvation is circumscribed by its
own formulas and creeds. This is not to say that we should
regard the traditional elements of Christianity as unimportant
—they are the central point of reference for this exposition.
And no matter how strange and incomprehensible many aspects of the biblical-Christian imagery—and especially the
figure of the Christ—may seem today (nor is the Church
blameless in this regard), this symbolism is the medium
through which the Christ has been made manifest in history.
If it is a meaningful symbolism, it will authenticate itself
through redemptive signs: it will reveal to man, as one ancient
Church father has suggested, his most profound being—his
being in the image of the Christ. Not where theology dismisses
the limitations of its own situation out of some peculiar com-
pulsion to make a virtue of necessity, but rather where it
incorporates them into its exposition, does the Church's proclamation justify its preaching, its teaching and counselling, its
mission to the heathen.

And if the ethical demand—the insistent question, What
ought I to do?—is linked by the Gospel of Jesus to the conception of the Christ, this conception also plays a major part
—both in its original statement and in its later reformulations
in Church dogmas—in answering the question of God developed in the previous chapter and at the beginning of this
present one. There it was suggested that the fatherhood of
God cannot be established solely from the perspective of the
creation, nor independently of the revelation of the Christ.
God was found to be a mystery calling forth our reverence,
but a mystery devoid of personality, a suprapersonal reality.
Only after we have come to know the Christ as a unique power
acting in the sphere of our personal lives and offering his

distinctive solution to the question, What ought I to do? can we appeal to God as the Father. Only through the Christ do we become aware of the creation's longing for redemption, do we even recognize the eschatological crisis and the answering grace which promises our salvation—the grace that originates in creative mystery and which through the Christ is transformed into the love of the Father for his children.

The sharp distinction drawn between the general revelation of God as creator, which provides some knowledge of God but does not plumb his most profound being, and the special revelation in Christ, through which our salvation is first disclosed, is clearly the strength of classical Catholic as well as orthodox Protestant dogmatics—in contrast to the premature explanation of God's fatherly compassion which earlier liberal theology thought it could discover in nature and in history.

For the New Testament does not speak in a general sense of God the Father, but always relates his activity and public manifestation to the eschatological work of redemption in Christ. And in turn, the Christ is for us a sign of that special experience in which our existence not only faces the crisis raised by the question, What ought I to do? but also is granted the redeeming answer and the strength to follow it as well. The mystery of God is not overcome through Christ—on the contrary, it is made the more profound in our eyes; for God must now be understood not only as the ground of being but as the meaning of our existence. No longer simply a terrifying mystery before which we must remain silent, God now becomes a blessed mystery and one to whom we can joyfully offer our praise.

If the questions raised earlier in this analysis regarding God and Christ seem to have been solved, immediately

4 New questions

arise—as much from general reflection about the meaning of human existence as from the Bible.

Even a momentary review of the Bible obliges us to ask, What is the present status of the kingdom of God? Have we not detached the biblical belief in redemption from its original cosmic dimension in redemptive history and converted it to a purely subjective human concern? Where in this wholly personal conception of redemption is the ultimate fulfillment hinted in the Bible? Is the kingdom of God no more than being-in-Christ? Must not the power of this New Being also prove itself in the realization of the kingdom of God? Is the world-historical significance of Christ not sacrificed if it is limited to the question, What ought I to do? Should not action be related to and perfected in the kingdom of God?

It is certainly true that the concept of the kingdom of God which stands at the center of the proclamation of Jesus conspicuously recedes in the writings of Paul and is almost totally absent in John. But did not even Paul expect the imminent second coming of Christ to establish his dominion, and does not the New Testament draw to a close with the fervent plea, "Come, Lord Jesus!"? Or is this expectation conclusively discharged by its non-realization? Is it merely to be considered the foolish hope of dreamers and visionaries? Must we relegate this hope to the fanatic or does it have a legitimate place in the future of the Christian faith? What can the notion of the kingdom of God mean for us today? What is the significance of redemptive history? Can we live comfortably without it? For what may we hope in the future?

And further questions arise from general deliberation about the meaning of human existence—quite apart from the biblical conception of God's kingdom. Is it possible, we must ask, to speak of a meaningful fulfillment of human existence without reference to history? Should not personal salvation take effect in history? Can personal experience be isolated from the process of history? Must it not somehow be established in relation to the meaning of being as a whole? Does the meaning of history not demand our attention as insistently as does the meaning of personal existence? What possible status can existence have if history as a whole, in which human existence is situated, has no meaning? Would such a conclusion not place in doubt the reality of personal redemption? Must the kingdom of God not be the meaning of history, if redemption in Christ is to be authentic? Is the creator-God not one with the redeemer-God? Thus general questioning merges again into the biblical problem of the coming of the kingdom of God.

Indeed, both biblical and non-biblical analyses of history raise the question of history's relation to the kingdom of God, and it is to this issue that our next chapter must be directed. For unless we attempt an answer to the problem of the kingdom of God and, concomitantly, to Kant's third question, What may I hope? we cannot claim to have spoken adequately of God the creator nor of our salvation in Christ.

But first—fully conscious of the limitations of what has been presented up to this point and at the same time aware of the magnitude of the problems raised by this third topic—let us close this chapter with a summary statement of Christ's meaning for us in the words of Paul: "But far be it from me to glory except in the cross of our Lord Jesus Christ, by which the world has been crucified to me, and I to the world" (Gal. 6:14).

Four

HISTORY AND THE

KINGDOM OF GOD

At the close of the last chapter we were obliged to ask How are we to understand the kingdom of God? and What is the meaning of history? Perhaps the Christ is the symbol of a possible redemptive reality; but even if this reality is understood as the creative grace of God and not as the invention of man, it has still been restricted in this analysis to the relatively narrow sphere of personal existence. Yet the New Testament acclaims the Christ as the harbinger of the kingdom of God, not simply as the redeemer of individuals. According to scripture, the kingdom will come as a mighty cosmic power transforming heaven and earth; it will break into history and signal its end; it will subdue the forces of evil in this world and bring it to pass that "God may be everything to everyone" (I Cor. 15:28).

If we acknowledge the primitive Christian expectation of the imminent fulfillment of the eschatological prediction to be an illusion and repudiate this hope as the New Testament's great blunder—a blunder subsequently perpetuated in the Church's theology of redemptive history—and if we further reject the Church's account of the beyond and speculation about ultimate perfection, what, then, is the meaning of history? Not only the authority of the Bible is at stake but also our response to the question, What ought I to do? Answers given to this question in previous eras in the form of responsible actions have yielded at least momentary meaning to history; surely man's acts can shape history. But just as surely,

man is sometimes confronted by forces which despite his
actions he cannot control, forces which, on the contrary, control him. Thus we are led again to ask, How can we realize
the meaning of personal existence if our individual designs
are not guaranteed by a significance for history as a whole?
Must we not be guided by *some* ultimate explanation of history
if our efforts are not to be condemned to failure from the
outset? Should we admit that there is no meaning in history
apart from our acts? Or should we try to interpret the ship-
wreck of the primitive Christian expectation manifested in the
cross of Jesus as the symbol of a possibly meaningful fulfillment for both human existence and history alike—a symbol
of the real beginning of God's kingdom, hidden to the mere
spectator, but continually dawning for its adopted members?

Such questions inevitably lead us to an analysis of the concepts of history and of God's kingdom, and in applying ourselves to these topics we must try to answer the old and ever
new question, What may I hope? for ours is an age as much in
need of hope as it is seemingly dedicated to futile expecta-
tions.[1]

If we proceed from what were established in the first chapter as the distinctive features of the intellectual complex of
our times—the collapse of faith in progress and the rediscovery
of the eschatological cast of the New Testament's conception
of the kingdom of God—we find that our present intellectual
climate is torn between a fatalistic attitude towards history
and a dubious confidence in redemptive history. We shall have
to show, then, what we cannot—but also need not—hope;
what, however, we can and ought to do, and also what may be
our legitimate hopes for the future in the light of an authentic
understanding of history and of God's kingdom.

[1] For a more detailed exposition of what follows see Fritz Buri, *"Vom
Sinn der Geschichte"* in *Schweiz Theol.* (1940), pp. 17 ff.

1 What we must grapple with in our time

is the fact that

A *We can no longer construct a comprehensive account of the development of history as a whole.*

In earlier periods comprehensive world views were a standard feature of historical analysis, but today we recognize the mythological character of such constructions not only in religious dogmatics but also in ostensibly philosophic and scientific formulations. We recognize that the true significance of such world views lies not in their objective spatial-temporal validity but rather in their vivid expression of man's self-consciousness, that a world view is less an account of external reality than a display of the inner man.

Thus, for instance, the great philosophic-historical systems of German idealism reconstructed the biblical myth of redemptive history after it had undergone transformations, of course, throughout antiquity and the Middle Ages. The appropriation of new concepts and the impact of modern scientific-historical attitudes notwithstanding, the basically mythological character of such constructions—and especially their debt to the biblical expectation of the end—is obvious. In these latter-day world views, as in the original biblical mythology, the world process unfolds towards a goal of absolute perfection. The only real difference between the ancient and modern versions of the myth is that the distinctive turning point for biblical redemptive history lies in God's supervention upon the world, whereas for philosophical idealism change evolves totally from within the historical process. Just as the Christ subjects himself to history in order to die for its conquest and the resurrection to a new life, the Absolute Spirit of idealism enters history, is estranged and annihilated by it, and through this self-denial overcomes reluctant matter and creates a new spiritual cosmos. Behind each formulation stands a powerful ethical drive towards absolute perfection of life and world.[2]

The consequences were as disastrous for idealism as for primitive Christian eschatology when its mythological world view was mistaken for a literal prediction—that is to say, when idealism thought it possible to view history as an ever higher evolution promoted by the instruments of modern culture and technology as when the kingdom of God was anticipated as an imminent historical event. The expected end failed to materialize for Christianity and the Church was substituted for God's kingdom: the earthquake of Lisbon and the social crises engendered by modern technology shook the foundations of idealism's optimism. New mythologies were developed —materialism, naturalism and pessimism—which would express man's self-understanding in terms once again appropriate to his experience, mythologies not in the least prone to the self-deceptions of previous world views. Perhaps Christian enthusiasm toward the kingdom of God and the modern optimism about progress gave legitimate expression to the self-understanding and native experience of their immediate proponents, but for us such positive attitudes are only another source of disillusionment and disappointment: the events of our time have forced us to abandon such sanguine schemata.

Certainly we can concede that it would be gratifying to find our loftiest hopes and noblest ideals guaranteed future fulfillment in this or a better world, if for no other reason than that they are lofty and noble. The primitive Christian expectation of the kingdom of God and modern faith in progress did

[2] See Emmanuel Hirsch, *Die Reichs-Gottes-Begriffe des neueren europäischen Denkens* (1921); Jacob Taubes, *Abendlandische Eschatologie* (Bern, A. Francke, 1947).

offer such assurance, and the loss engendered by the shattering of these illusions may prove to be devastating. So long as such hopes were alive they could both sustain the believer in the face of doubt and offer him practical guides to action. Men could work for what they thought was expected of them with the sense that their lives were being lived in accordance with the will of God or with the intention of the universe. Humanity was convinced that a just God ruled and that the world was meaningfully ordered, that the Good would ultimately triumph in history. Recalcitrant evil only endured to be overcome; certainly, it was felt, it would be overcome. Thus modern evolutionary optimism proved a powerful stimulus to ethical activity. Perhaps, when contrasted with the expectation of the kingdom of God, secular idealism seems a stark reduction to worldly terms of man's highest aspirations. Yet because the world was comprehended in terms of evolutionary progress, the secular world view of idealism certainly promoted powerful ethical drives. The loss of such ethical concern is an all too apparent result of the collapse of previous optimistic outlooks; today we are beset by doubts and by an overpoweringly chaotic sense of hopelessness, and we have become more sober and poorer in spirit as a consequence. The apparent objective realities as well as the comforting mysteries of an earlier age now taunt us as subjective fancies which have abandoned us to a wilderness. We stand once more with Nietzsche:

> The rook cries out
> And draws the soaring flocks to the city:
> Soon it will snow:
> Woe to him who has no home!

If in the face of such despair we would still place our trust in hymns to the eternal peace of the heavenly city, or in the watchwords of cultural protestantism's kingdom of God on earth, we must explain the fact that

B   *In the New Testament the kingdom of God signifies*
neither a heavenly beyond nor an earthly cultural goal.

In his repudiation of all worlds beyond the present one,
Nietzsche actually stood nearer the biblical position than
many who were piously shocked by his "Brothers, place your
faith in this world." For the kingdom of God was proclaimed
by the New Testament as an ultimate power and not the static
heaven of Christianity, eternally unchanging, turned in upon
itself. The kingdom's function was rather to break in upon
human history and to change the world. "Corporeality," as
it was later formulated, is actually "the way of God." The
doctrine of immortality is a conception taken over from pagan
antiquity by early Christianity, and one which is totally foreign to the Bible. The Old Testament is candidly bleak in its
statements about life after death; the dead cannot praise God
and lead only a pitiful, shadowy existence in the underworld.

Developed independently of the Bible, the doctrine of immortality was adopted by Christianity in order to guarantee
personal existence after death in the face of rising doubts
about redemption. Originally the expectation of redemption
had been grounded solely in the hope of participation in the
kingdom of God expected to dawn imminently for God's elect
on earth. Only desperation about its own political fate had
encouraged the rise in late Judaism of the doctrine of resurrection taken over by the New Testament. And it was only in the
New Testament that resurrection achieved its close relationship to the expectation of God's kingdom. Jesus promised his
own that they would sit at his table in the kingdom and that
they would one day undergo judgment.

The non-fulfillment of Jesus' promise in the death of individual believers before the advent of the kingdom produced
severe tensions in the first Christian community. "Where is the
promise of his coming? For ever since the fathers fell asleep,
all things have continued as they were from the beginning of

creation" (II Peter 3:4). Disappointment was especially pro-
nounced where the lordship of Christ was thought to precede
the kingdom of God for an extended period, for instance, the
thousand-year reign of Revelation 20. Consequently, it was
maintained that believers who had died before the end would
be excluded from the kingdom only until death should be
conquered at the end of the era. The apostle Paul solved this
dilemma with his explanation that baptised believers would
not be obliged to wait until the general resurrection but would
be raised with the second coming of the Lord. Together with
those believers who would experience this event during their
lifetimes and be transformed by it, the baptised dead would
directly enter the messianic kingdom (I Thess. 4:13 ff.). Related to this first partial resurrection at the reappearance of
Christ is Paul's well-known exposition in I Corinthians 15:
the spiritual body is created in baptism and lives in the old
frame of the physical body; it is the spiritual body which will
be resurrected at the beginning of the ultimate event and
whose bearer need not wait until the day of judgment.

The early Christian resurrection hope, which has only
been recounted here in outline,[3] is a radically different conception than the doctrines of immortality and the "beyond"
into which the original biblical understanding was subsequently recast. Such "development" of doctrine—already apparent in the Gospel of John—was necessitated by history's
prolongation, by the postponement of the end. Early Christian
eschatology could offer no adequate answer to the questions
raised regarding the fate of those who had already died. Thus,
faith in Christ's dominion from afar—since this dominion did
not seem readily apparent in the world of the Church—was
replaced by faith in a supramundane beyond, a tripartite
realm of immortal souls—a heaven, a hell and a purgatory.
But as much as the Church embellished this beyond with im-

[3] For fuller details see the appropriate chapters in Albert Schweitzer's
The Mysticism of Paul the Apostle.

agined detail, it was still found difficult to justify according
to Scripture; for the imminent kingdom of God which one
enters by resurrection—or by transfiguration if one is still alive
at its advent—is something other than the heaven invented by
antiquity and subsequently expounded by Christianity—a beyond in which the immortal soul might elude extinction by
lingering at some way station while awaiting the advent of a
vaguely adumbrated end.

No less a modification of the original significance of the
kingdom was the expectation prescribed by the modern era—
particularly the cultural striving of the nineteenth century
which replaced the older belief in a heavenly beyond. This
modern understanding of God's kingdom as a perfected human
society corresponded to the disintegration of the three-storied
universe of the Middle Ages—heaven, earth and underworld;
attention was redirected to the present life and as one exponent, Feuerbach, proclaimed at the conclusion of his *Vor-
lesung über das Wesen der Religion:* "To abandon the beyond
is to affirm the present world for its own sake: our repudiation
of a 'better life in heaven' signals the advent of progress now—
progress which will improve life on earth, and transform a
frivolous, unproductive object of faith into an immediate goal
of duty, an impetus to human activity."

Without renouncing immortality and supernatural perfection, cultural protestantism of the nineteenth and early twentieth centuries also came to understand the kingdom of God as
an ideal to be realized by human effort. The present labor of
God's kingdom was proclaimed and history pursued as the
broad way towards an earthly paradise, a Christian world, the
realization of the kingdom on earth.

Undoubtedly something of the fire of the primitive Christian
expectation of the kingdom was active in this cultural enthusiasm. Culture was not seen as an excuse for complacent delay
until the advent of a future life, nor was it viewed as a pre-

mature refuge for the faithful; rather culture became a forced march towards the beginning of the kingdom in the present age, a march demanding the active participation of every true believer. But if Jesus kindled the will for repentance directed towards the kingdom of God and went to his death in order to bring this kingdom into being, if Paul based his missionary activity on his assumption that the Gospel must be preached in all lands before the advent of the kingdom, still the biblical authors never assumed that the kingdom would be the product of human effort. However it might promote active response on man's part, the kingdom was conceived as a supernatural event to be brought about by God's power alone. In Paul's understanding, the kingdom's supernatural perfection was rather a judgment upon all human acts than the motivating impulse towards some cultural goal. Such is the real lesson of the New Testament's eschatology—even apart from the humbling of modern cultural faith in the crisis of recent political catastrophes. Surely our own experience can only strengthen the original eschatological understanding of God's kingdom.

In sum, we must come to terms with the fact that we can neither formulate an independent conception of the development of history as a whole nor ultilize either the other-worldliness or this-worldliness of the primitive Christian understanding of the kingdom of God for such a purpose. Before we present our own response to the spiritual crisis of our time, however, we must analyze

2   The conclusions of other movements with
which we cannot agree.

The first such unacceptable conclusion is

A   *Naturalism's sacrifice of the meaning of history in its*
pessimistic attitude towards the creative powers of the
human spirit.

In our earlier analysis of the characteristic features of the
face of our time we noted the naturalistic reduction of the
meaning of history. According to naturalism, spiritual significance can no longer be attributed to history, the powers of
God and man alike are reduced to natural phenomena—sometimes seen as organic, sometimes mechanistic in nature, sense-
lessly chaotic if not positively destructive in consequences
("The Spirit as the Adversary of the Soul").[4]

If some de-emphasis of the role of human or divine spiritual
powers at work in history is justified, naturalism's critique,
which views history only as a mechanism compelled to operate
by meaningless drives, goes astray when it totally denies
history's spiritual significance. Nor is this tendency dissimilar
to the distortion involved in the reduction of God and his
powers to the level of personal struggle against the forces of
this world—as if the creator only acted and conquered according to human standards of good and evil, or as if evil itself did
not also originate out of God's creative ground. Again, if too
much confidence has been placed in the "world principles" and

[4] This is the title of a well-known book by Ludwig Klages (*Der Geist
als Widersacher der Seele*) which has become nearly as much a catch-
phrase as Oswald Spengler's *The Decline of the West* mentioned earlier.

cultural creations of human society, just as inappropriately has naturalism identified God and world as one and denied the realities of human freedom and responsibility.

The pantheistic merger of God and world which is always connected in some way or another with the organic interpretation of history (and also pantheism which further depresses God merely to one force among others operating within the world) contradicts what we attempted to amplify in the second chapter regarding the relationship of God and the world. The notion of God's bondage to the world is antithetical to our sense of createdness, the sense which reminds us that we are dependent upon a power which we cannot comprehend within our normal categories of understanding. This sense of our own limitations prohibits any attempt to confine God's mystery to the sphere of worldly understanding.

Just as the recognition that our freedom and responsibility are grounded in the being of God is related to our sense of the limitations of our createdness—a connection which can lead to the feeling that we are determined rather than free and responsible, or "damned" as current philosophy has put it [5]—so from the standpoint of naturalistic pantheism, ethical concerns may be threatened by fatalism, the surrender to an incomprehensible and immutable sense of destiny. Religious pessimism does at least appear to be immune to pantheism's irrational, Promethean need to console man, its amoral drive towards self-deification. But despite the vast contrast in their effects—resigned submission to pathetic tragedy on the one hand, glorification of the will to power on the other—equally ominous views of history are currently exemplified by each of these perspectives. Their common and basic error—just as for their Christian-idealistic predecessors—lies in their attempt to construct a uniform and comprehensive view of history, its essence and development admittedly not powered by the

[5] Jean Paul Sartre, *Existentialism*, trans. by Bernard Frechtman (New York, Philosophical Library, 1947).

spiritual optimism of the past but now by pessimistic, natural-istic despair regarding any hope for a better future. Just as Christian idealism sought to de-emphasize the absurd and evil aspects of history, Christian pessimism dismisses the equally mysterious creative power of the spirit. Instead of being grasped as the riddle and wonder of history, the spirit—just as in Christian idealism's view of history—is made the sub-structure of an empty scaffolding. If formerly the spirit was submerged under the debris of arrogant systems, it is shackled now by chains which it has been allowed to impose on itself. We must guard against this second danger no less than the first, reject the pessimism of naturalism as firmly as the opti-mism of idealism. In each instance we are confronted with an untenable view of history and one which operates with dis-astrous effect.

No less dubious in its bases than in its consequences is

B   *The renewed construction of a redemptive history on the alleged foundations of supernatural revelation.*

As current orthodox revelation theology believes that athe-ism and nihilism are the inevitable outgrowth of unbelief, so it interprets the naturalistic sacrifice of history as a direct conse-quence of secular historical viewpoints. The self-analysis of natural man, it maintains, can only lead to the building of a new tower of Babel, and after its collapse, to a Babylonian confusion of tongues. Left to his own devices, natural man will overrate himself and history in ruinous fashion, or else, no less destructively, underestimate them. Only on the basis of Chris-tian revelation is it thought possible to recognize history as the domain of that being which can decide to be "neither angel nor beast." [6]

Our response to revelation theology is not to deny that the Bible—and especially its conception of the kingdom of God—

[6] Pascal, *Pensées*, No. 140.

sheds light on the meaning of history, nor to deny that it can provide an authentic historical understanding. What must be rejected in revelation theology is its reduction of history to an external shell, and further, its belief that it can appeal to Scripture for supernatural sanction of its views.

The uncertain status of this alleged foundation of revelation is all too apparent. We have observed how the biblical expectation of the imminent realization of the kingdom of God became a source of disappointment for early Christianity as the course of history was prolonged. Further, this hope, itself, was not unique but is shared by other religious traditions; it can be given naturalistic explanations by secular history or by psychology of religion. Yet it was precisely the discovery that the New Testament's expectation of the end was an illusion that induced the Church to elevate Scripture to a supernatural status. Consequently, the Church came to make assertions about history which were not based on natural experience but, on the contrary, directly contradicted it. If the New Testament proclamation is to be retained for the sake of salvation, it must be rescued from such untenable resistance to natural knowledge. It is supposed that the quality of supernatural revelation can be ascribed to the Scriptures; yet such an assertion depends upon a faith which itself presupposes the supernatural character of the original revelation. If such circular reasoning is to be the basis for the assertion of the supernatural character of revelation (as the psychology of religion as well as the history of dogma would seem to indicate) then the theology of redemptive history is deprived of its right of appeal to supernatural revelation as the source of its authority. It accordingly stands on the same plane as all other theologies; its attempts to formulate a meaningful explanation of history must be attributed to thoroughly natural motives common to the history of the spirit. In contrast to the faith in evolution of progress-idealism or the pessimism of pantheistic naturalism, Christian eschatology certainly proclaims a distinctive significance for history, and this significance (as we must shortly demonstrate) is inherently superior to other types that we have discussed. However, eschatology does not for this reason escape the general context of human intellectual history.

Precisely because theology of redemptive history claims absolute, divine authority for its schemata—creation, fall, old and new covenant, the dominion of Christ initiated with his ascension and reappearance at the day of judgment—the risks inherent in its external formulations are all the more acute. If objective validity is claimed for idealism and naturalism rather than their being valued as expressions of human self-consciousness, and if in consequence, they are used to distort reality and to generate destructive ideological power struggles, so in incomparably greater measure does an ideology which claims divine authority for itself risk major blunders. Church history and the history of doctrine as well as the current condition of the Church offer only too many illustrations of such painful errors. When the Church, only a human institution, directly or in some dialectical fashion claims divine authority for itself and its dogmas, its fruits are too frequently the demonic rather than the sanctified, intolerance and not community—sins which are hardly the heritage of Roman Catholicism alone.

Thus, we must reject redemptive history's appeal to the eschatological proclamation of the New Testament just as firmly as we repudiated the secularization of eschatology by idealism and its abrogation by naturalism.

Now that we have educed how we must come to terms with current views of the kingdom of God and recognized how we cannot legitimately interpret it, we can propound

3 The implications of the primitive Christian expectation of the kingdom of God for our own understanding of history

Earlier, the biblical conception of the creator was offered as an answer to the question, How can we speak of God? and the original figure of the Christ became a symbol for the reality of redemption. Similarly, the primitive Christian expectation of God's kingdom—along with the continuation of its problematic development in history—can now be disclosed as that for which we should hope in the future. But let us begin by stating this solution in negative form since

A *The kingdom of God is manifested as the crisis of history and history as the crisis of the kingdom of God.*

Even in their day, the Hebrew prophets depicted the kingdom of God as a supernatural power: its fulfillment would bring judgment on all humanity—even "the high and the mighty." [7] All the more did Jesus and his community interpret the kingdom of God as a supernatural event. All national and worldly boundaries would be transcended by the kingdom; its dominion would extend throughout the whole cosmos. The kingdom would break into history—as its radical replacement, not as its extension. Perhaps man had already entered a new era which had begun to affect his natural condition—but no part of this drama of the end of time was viewed as the

[7] This understanding is acutely and impressively grasped and expressed by Paul Tillich. See, for instance, his collection of essays, *The Protestant Era* (Chicago, University of Chicago Press, 1948).

product of human activity. The judgment on men would
come, but when and how would be determined according to
God's will. Man would have to stand the test of God's judgment, but only election by God would prove human merit.

This is a much different view than that of Thomas Aquinas,
who maintained that grace does not destroy nature but only
increases and perfects it. The primitive community believed
that nature would be superseded and that a new being would
take the place of the old in the cosmic as well as in the human
sphere: there will be a new heaven and a new earth; there will
be a new creature in Christ. Of the form of the world, it was
said that it shall pass away; and of natural man, "all have
sinned, and come short of the glory of God" (Rom. 3:23). The
kingdom of God thus in every way portends the crisis of
natural world history and all its potentialities. To try to calcu-
late its character further would be unreasonable (I Cor. 2:6
ff.). So far as one ventures to discuss it, one can only conclude
with the sense of those who "have as though they had none"
(I Cor. 7:29 ff.). Satan has already been overthrown (Luke
10:18), and from the outermost regions of the cosmos to the
most intimate personal decision a crisis is making its effects
known—the crisis that signals the first irruption of God's
kingdom into the existing world.

Such a crisis would not adequately characterize the actual
state of our world today if it were proclaimed only in terms of
the assumptions of the New Testament or as it reflects the
attitudes of the devout, that is, if the additional crisis that this
proclamation itself faces each moment that history is exended
were neglected. Such a crisis of the conception of the kingdom
of God in its national-political form beleaguered the external
destiny of the Jews and led eventually to the reformulated
universal-cosmic pronouncement of late Judaism. And such
a crisis in the non-fulfillment of the end conditioned its proclamation in the New Testament. The indirect effects of this non-
fulfillment are manifest in the emergence of the conception
of Jesus' suffering atonement (Matt. 16:21), in the announce-

ment to the disciples of the kingdom's imminent advent and the universal afflictions to be anticipated with it on their return from their first missionary journey (Matt. 10:21), in the uncertainty of the apostle Paul as to whether or not he would personally experience the end (Phil. 1:23) and in the subsequent explanation of the delay in terms of the psalmist's reflection that with God a thousand years are as a day—that postponement did not abrogate the promise (II Pet. 3:4 ff). Such examples betray the crisis which affected the Gospel as it was confronted by the unanticipated prolongation of history —the crisis which stamped indelibly the contents of the proclamation itself. In the subsequent history of Christianity this crisis has always become manifest wherever the primitive Christian expectation of the imminent end has been applied to contemporary history. Repeatedly this expectation has not only brought unrest into the world, but has itself become suspect through its nonfulfillment. From the disappointment in the time of Zerubbabel to Golgotha where Jesus expired with the cry, "My God, my God, why hast thou forsaken me?" —for the visionaries of the Church past and present this crisis of expectation has extended throughout history.[8]

In this double crisis—the crisis which the kingdom of God signifies for history since it reveals its lack of completion; and the crisis which history causes the expectation of the kingdom of God since it belies its fulfillment—the essential characteristics of the eschatological interpretation of history become apparent. History is not conceived as a process directed towards the realization of its meaning as a whole—such as was the case in progress optimism—but rather each moment in history is understood as a unique event, similar in kind to the world-annihilating final cataclysm in which history's consummation will be realized. An ultimate fulfillment cannot take place in the dimension of world history: it founders in the real world. But it is in the real world that the so-called re-

[8] See Walter Nigg's *Das ewige Reich, Geschichte einer Sehnsucht und einer Enttäuschung* (Erlewbach-Zürich, E. Rentsch, 1944).

demptive event is manifest and thus reveals itself to be a phenomenon of world history after all, and not the supernatural, divine, occurrence suggested by redemptive history. The fact that the ideal of the kingdom of God emerges in history and still survives despite its complete historical failure also discloses the error of pessimistic naturalism which can discover in history only meaningless forces at work. With the realization in history of the concept of the kingdom of God a new historical factor appears which manifests its power over history. History turns out to be directed towards a goal which can no longer be understood to justify or guarantee itself; for any attempt to characterize the kingdom of God as the comprehensive meaning of history immediately betrays the kingdom as well as the utmost possibilities of history which consist in the recognition that history can be questioned for the sake of its perfection and can bear the risk of its non-fulfillment. Only in this way can the crisis of the kingdom of God become the completion of history in each new era.[9]

This completion, however, cannot be circumscribed by any idealistic or redemptive historical vision of the future. If it is expressed in such limited terms it again becomes an illusion. The fulfillment of the kingdom is only possible where the crisis irrupts into history at a particular place and time and issues in thought and action. What is meant by all this can be expressed in terms of

B *Christian culture as a possible meaning of history.*

Our hope for the future can be directed towards the possibility of Christian culture. We possess no guarantee of the fulfillment of this hope—neither in humanism nor in idealism, nor in supernatural redemptive history. Idealism fails to recognize the incomprehensibility of history and betrays the eschatological crisis through its absolutization of cultural systems. Theology of redemptive history, for its part, irrationally sacrifices the possibilities of history to a supposed divine plan

[9] See Karl Jaspers, *The Origin and Goal of History* (London, Routledge & Kegan Paul, Ltd., 1953).

of redemption. Inherent in the breakdown of both these positive constructions is their offspring, naturalistic pessimism. In
answer to this latter view, however, we suggest that in Christian faith as we have attempted to propound it meaning can
be discovered, and that in such meaning can be glimpsed the
renewal of history in its original sense as the creation of
culture.

For this reason we would direct attention once again to
what was said earlier about the biblical conception of the
creator. We discovered in this conception a means of expression for that ultimate understanding of reality—sometimes
revealed to us directly, sometimes as the consequence of
much reflection—which perceives that being in its fullest sense
is incomprehensible, a mode of understanding which dissipates
rather than answers our questions regarding the creative mystery of God, which redirects our attention to our own createdness.

Such an understanding of God and of ourselves is consider-
ably more than a theoretical conclusion: the perception of
God as creator and of our own existence as creatures is of the
greatest practical import. We cannot secure this awareness in
a formula so as to manipulate it theoretically—such an understanding rather engrosses our whole being: I am a creature
and all that surrounds me is also the product of creation; it
does not lie under my power.

> God is present
> Let us worship
> And walk before him in awe!

We do not simply persevere in reverent silence but are commanded, as the mystic Teersteeger once said, "Give your heart
to him anew!"—live out of your awe and acknowledge that all
you encounter stands reverently before the creative mystery
that it reveals.[10]

[10] Perhaps in this fashion Albert Schweitzer's concept of "reverence
for life" may be extended. See Fritz Buri, *Christentum und Kultur bei
Albert Schweitzer* (1941).

In the concept of awe or reverence we discover an ethical principle which does not depend on alien authority, which need not arduously prove its authenticity to us, but which is constantly rediscovered in each extension of our analysis of experience. Without it I am not a person; my life is inauthentic. I can only live according to the truth reflected in my wonder before the mystery of createdness. Reverence for life is a part of my own humanity; it liberates me from bondage to nature so that I may enter the domain of history. Through it I become responsible, able to ask myself whether and how I should let myself be directed by this reverence in my attitudes and approach towards myself and towards my environment. It certainly does not obviate my power of decision, nor does it provide any basis for a "system" of ethics. Such schematization would encourage false security in the face of the unconditioned quality of its demands, would betray its significance, and I would experience such betrayal as tormenting self-contradiction. Yet even my guilt belongs to my humanity and my history. Nature knows no shame; only man in the context of history can experience it.

Nevertheless, we can neither produce nor prove this awareness of God—our reverence and our shame. We can only offer the evidence for it of our own experience in the hope that its reality and meaning will be disclosed to others as it has been to us. Nor can we construct from such an awareness a general system for history of an idealistic or redemptive historical stamp. Precisely the characteristic property of this experience is that it is not a universal reality, that it does not stand at our disposal, nor—where it manifests itself—can it even be represented as God's will or as the full meaning of his creation. To express the significance of this reality for our personal existence where its meaning is discovered in crisis, we have used the concept of special revelation in Christ. And where thought and action derive from the reality of Christ, we have suggested there will flourish what may truly be designated Christian culture.

Such Christian culture, however, so far as the regulation and the goals of history are concerned, is not some ultimate aim of historical development, nor a sign of supernatural perfection at the end of time. Christian culture is the continuously present possibility emergent from the crisis of each new epoch, a possibility that justifies itself as it yields new significance to the shape of life and new purposefulness to the surrounding world.

It is in crisis, then, that the kingdom of God begins. One such crisis was the subject of Jesus' proclamation, "Repent for the kingdom of God is at hand" (Matt. 4:17). We no longer need await the kingdom of God with the misguided literalness of the eschatological mythology; rather eschatology today, as it touches upon our personal fate after death and the future of mankind as a whole, can only hint of the unlimited possibilities of God's creation. These divine potentialities explode every human scheme; they offer infinitely greater grounds for hope than any human ideal or redemptive dogma—programs which only account for a limited aspect of God's creation and the new creation in Christ.

Such a perspective implies that the nature and tasks of the Church are limited: first, the Church must preserve the great symbols which are entrusted to it by the traditional accounts of the divine reality and bring them alive through sensible exposition. Second, the Church can be a society of individuals who have come to understand the Christian symbols in terms of their own experience, who have glimpsed the truth and reality of the kingdom of God in our time and embodied it in repentance and readiness for Christ. Where the Church claims greater functions for its organizations and institutions, it subverts its own proclamation and becomes—yes, even at my hand or yours—the domain of the anti-Christ. But where it proclaims true repentance and readiness for Christ, it merits the promise that the gates of hell shall not prevail against it (Matt. 16:18).

We are

4 In conclusion

aware that this exposition has not even touched upon many questions involved in the topic of Christian faith in our time. But it is hoped that at least the basic elements of what we believe can and must be proclaimed as Christian faith may have become apparent.

In response to the atheism, nihilism and naturalism confronting our time we offer the biblical conception of creation as an adequate expression of the mystery of being in which all our conceptual knowledge discovers its ultimate limits.

In the eschatological Christ, particularly as he was understood by Jesus and his apostle Paul, we find the symbol of the special possibilities inherent for man in the free gift of love between God and man.

And in the kingdom of God we discover the domain in which the creation of God is realized as history in its true sense—history always pointing beyond itself.

We hope this exposition has shed light not only on the momentary truths grasped by the perishable movements of our age—indefensible idealistic and redemptive historical fabrications—but also that it has set a positive course toward the conquest of the unique dilemmas of our time.

Can the Christian faith be valid for our time? "This is the victory that overcomes the world, our faith" (I John 5:4).